KINDER KOLLEGE
Math
(Primary Arithmetic)

Pre-K and Kindergarten

L. M. Logan
Patrice Juah
Ophelia S. Lewis

Village Tales Publishing

MINNEAPOLIS, MN

Copyright © 2020 by Liberia Literary Society

All rights reserved. No part of this publication may be reproduced, distributed or transmitted in any form or by any means, without prior written permission.

Village Tales Publishing
www.villagetalespublishing.com
www.oass.villagetalespublishing.com
www.villagetalespublishing.com/childrensbooks

Book Cover by OASS
ISBN-13 9781945408304
LCCN 2020904395

A Liberia Literary Society
Educational Project

Printed in the USA

This book belongs to:

_____

How to care for your book.

1. Read with clean hands.
2. Turn pages carefully.
3. Keep your book in your bookbag when you're not reading it.
4. Keep your book close to you when reading, so that you don't drop it.
5. Use a bookmark to save your page in a book.
6. Keep your book away from food and drinks.
7. Only draw, write, and color where instructed to.

Primary Arithmetic

The first thing I do is always the same,
I pick up my pencil and write my name.

  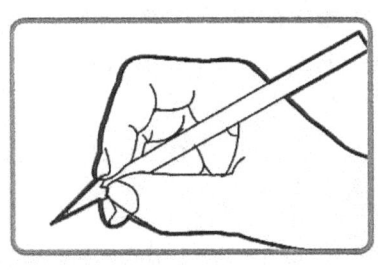

| Sit down and place book flat in front of you. | Use your helper hand to hold the paper down while writing. | Correctly hold your pencil; only move the fingers when writing. |

Contents

Math and Numbers 9
Math Shows How Numbers Work 10
Numbers Starts With Zero 11
Write the missing number 22
Number Words 22
Number Words Match 33
I Can Write to Twenty 36
I Can Write to Thirty 37
I Can Write to Forty 39
I Can Write to Fifty 41
Missing Numbers 43
I Can Count by 2s 45
I Can Count by 5s 46
I Can Count by 10s 47
1 - 100 Chart 48
Number Recognition 53
Color and Count 54
Which Number is Larger? 58
Greater Than / Less Than 62
Addition Word List 64
Counters 67
Count the Dots 68
Domino Addition 71
Addition 72
Solve the Problems 74
Missing Numbers 77
Tell the Truth 79
Seeing Double 83
Subtraction Word List 84
Take Away 85
Subtraction Facts 87

Shapes	92
Color by Sides	96
Color by Shape	97
Shape Sort	98
2D and 3D Shapes	100
Everyday 3D Shapes	101
Number Order	105
Ordinal Numbers	106
Passage of Time Order	107
Days of the Week	108
Preposition	110
Occupying Space	112
Left and Right Position	113
Capacity	116
Weight	117
Height	118
Width	119
Length	120
Think & Talk	122
Comparing Objects Size	123
Biggest	124
Smallest	125
Problem Solving	127
Time	129
All About Time	130
Telling Time	132
What Time is it?	133
Digital Clock	135
Word Problems	136
I Can Show My Thinking	139
Color and Count	147
Comparing Amounts	148
Before and After Numbers	150
Primary Color Mixing	154

Money 156
Currency & Money 157
Word Problems With LRDs (L$) 158
Coins and Bills 160
What We Do With Our Money 161
Math Crossword Puzzles 163

Math and Numbers

I have to know my numbers
so I can learn math.

I have to know my numbers
so I can count.

I have to know my numbers
to know how much money I have.

Math Shows How Numbers Work

Math tell us how many things we have.

Zaq has 2 new toys.
I have 3 cupcakes.

Math shows the size of something.

The cat is only 7 inches long.
This giraffe is 10 feet tall.

Math lets us know how far a place is.

Monrovia is three miles away.

Monrovia

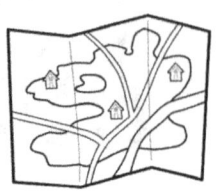

Numbers Starts With Zero

zero

I am holding zero pens in my hand.
I have nothing.

Trace the numbers, count the dots, and color each picture to match the sentence.

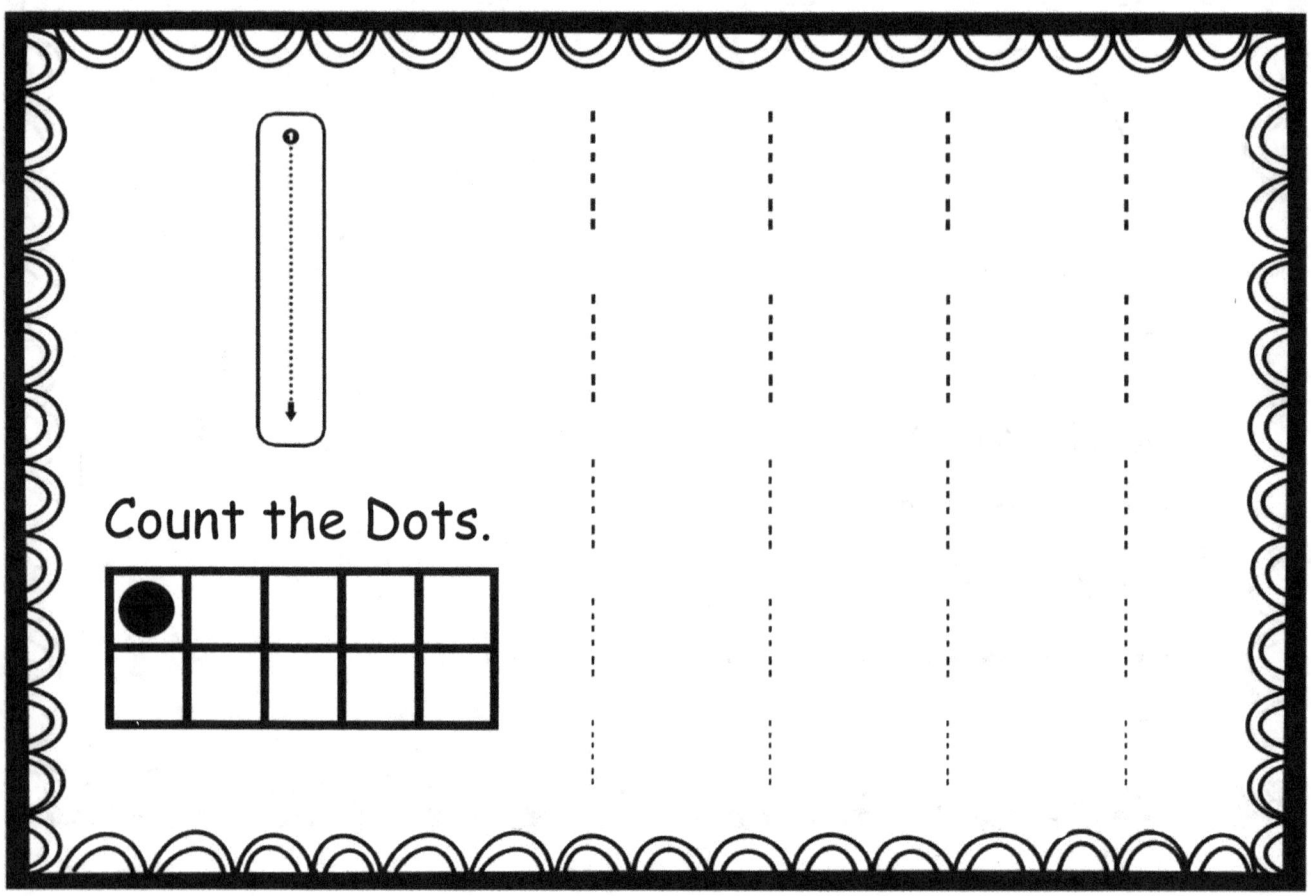

 I see one brown rabbit.

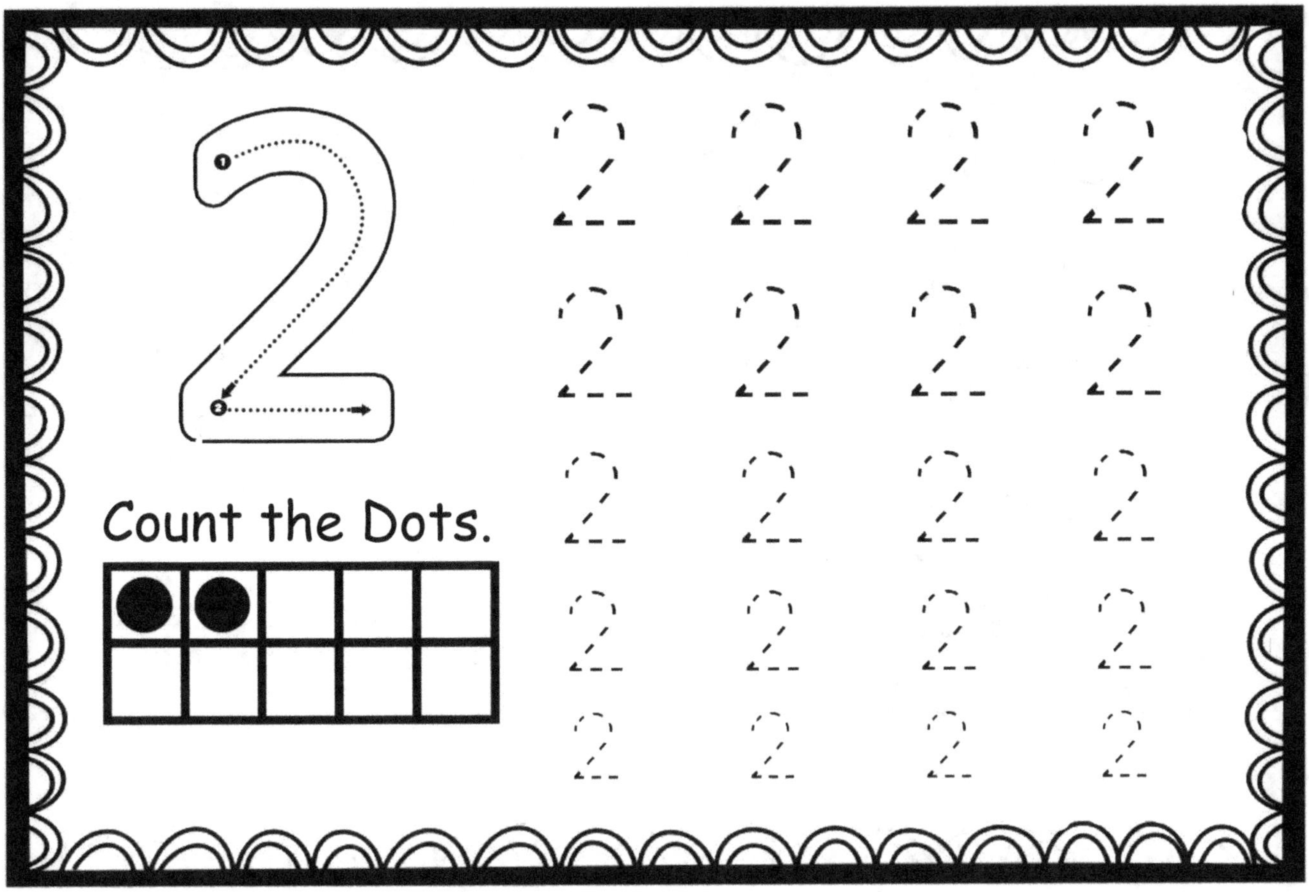

2

Count the Dots.

  There are two yellow butterflies.

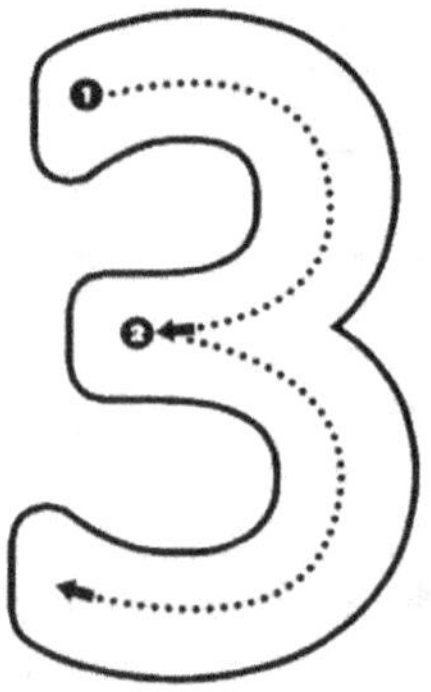

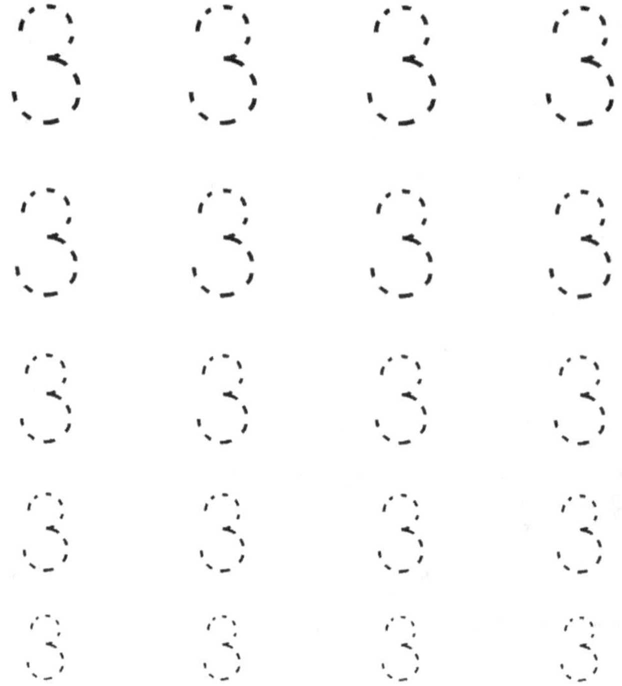

Count the Dots.

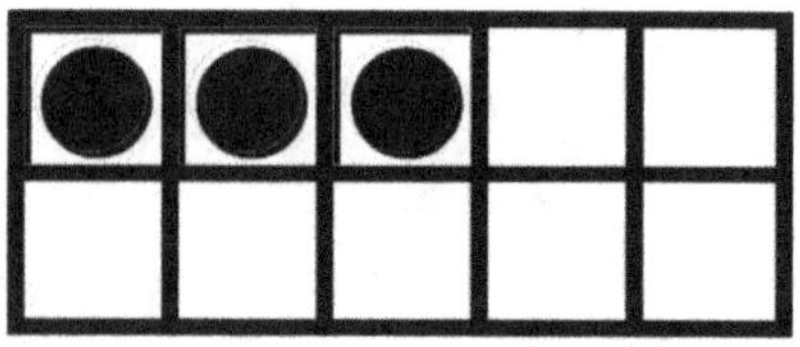

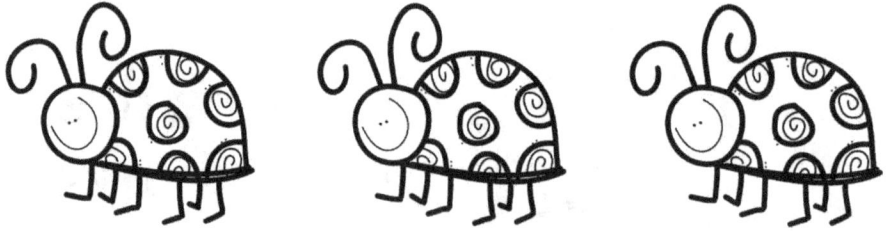

Three red Ladybugs are racing.

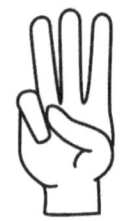

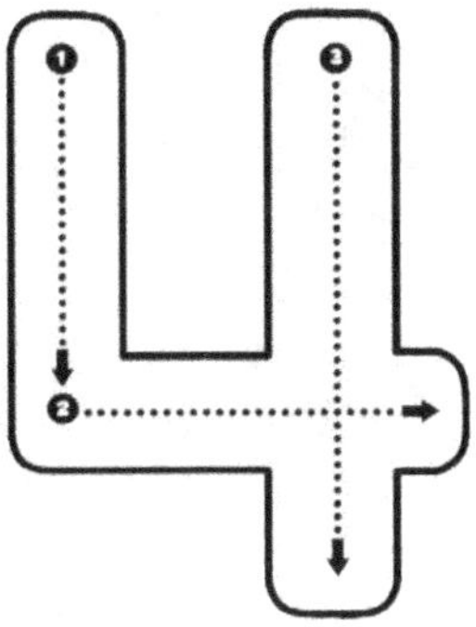

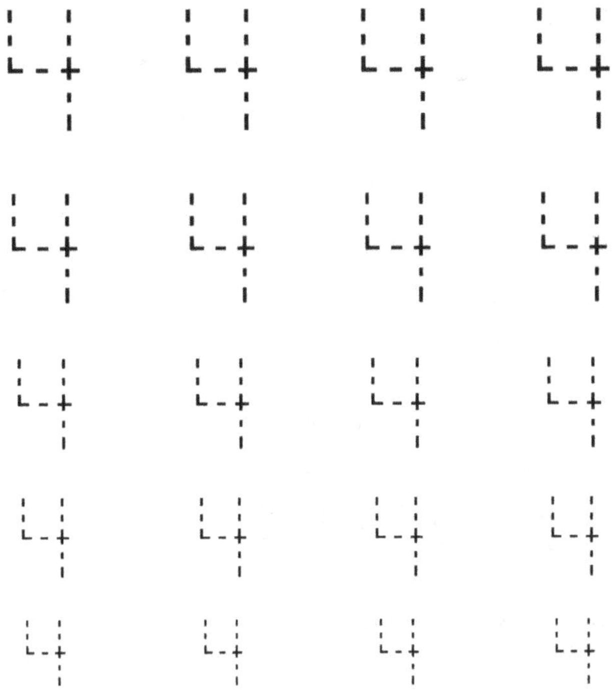

4

Count the Dots.

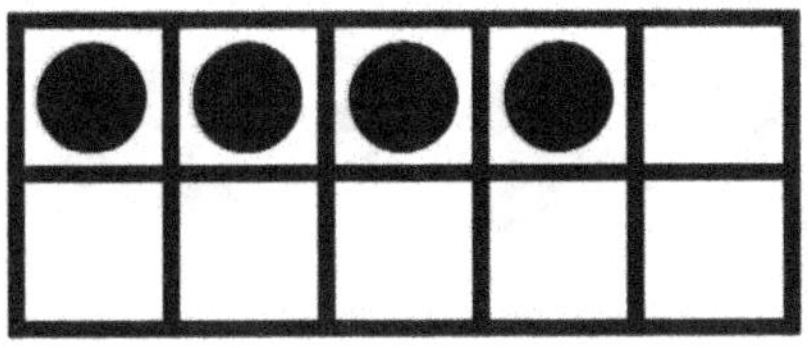

4	4	4	4
4	4	4	4
4	4	4	4
4	4	4	4
4	4	4	4

I have four green gifts for Musu.

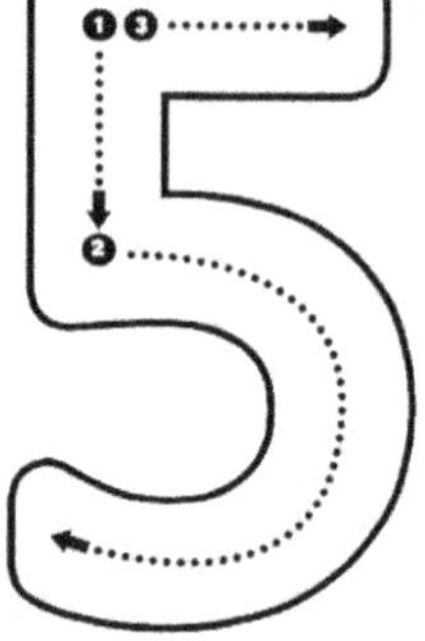

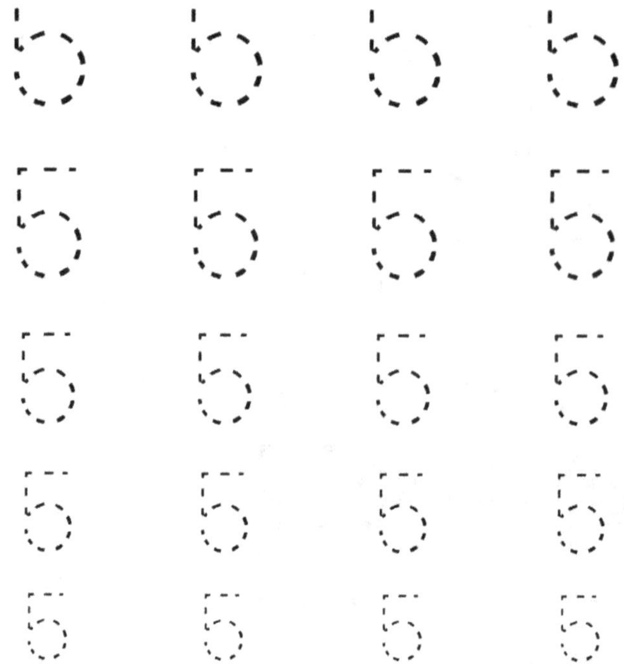

Count the Dots.

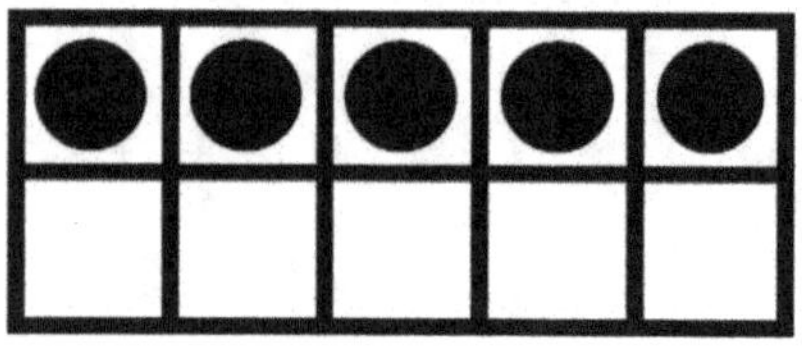

Are these five blue birds friends?

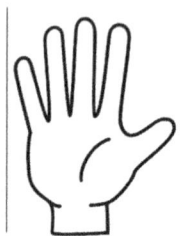

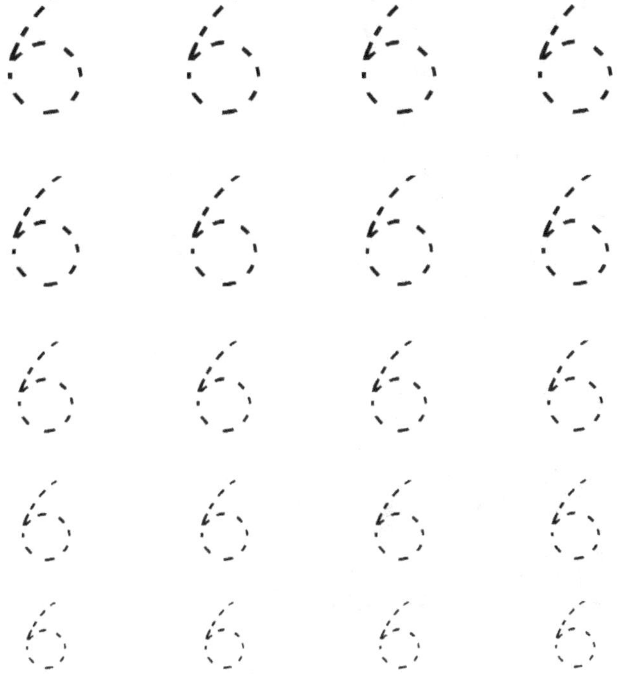

Count the Dots.

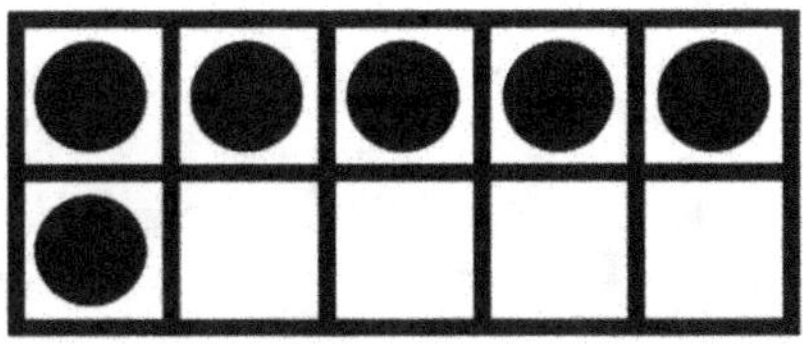

Color six petals purple.

17

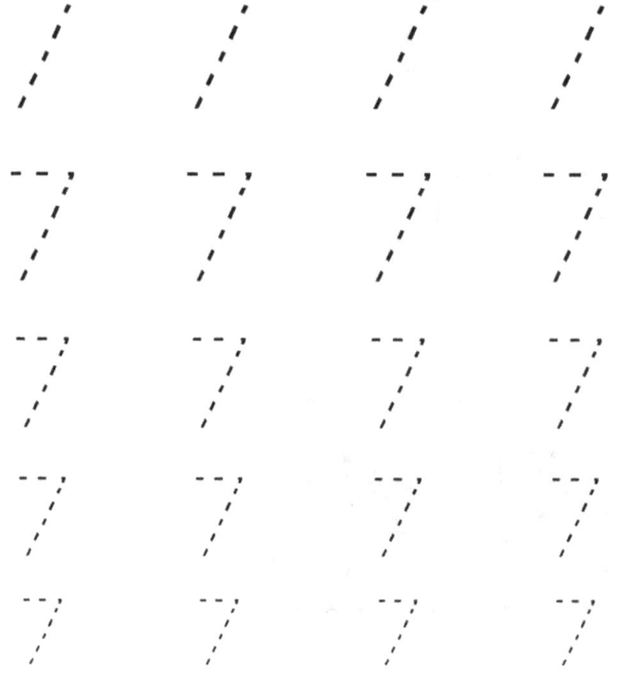

7

Count the Dots.

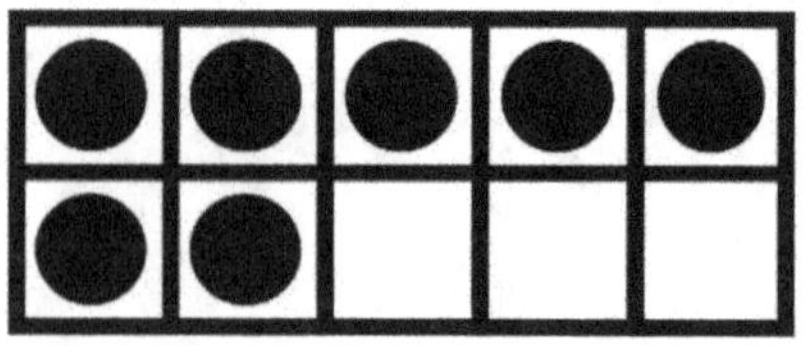

Zaq has seven toy boats. He has three red boats and four green boats.

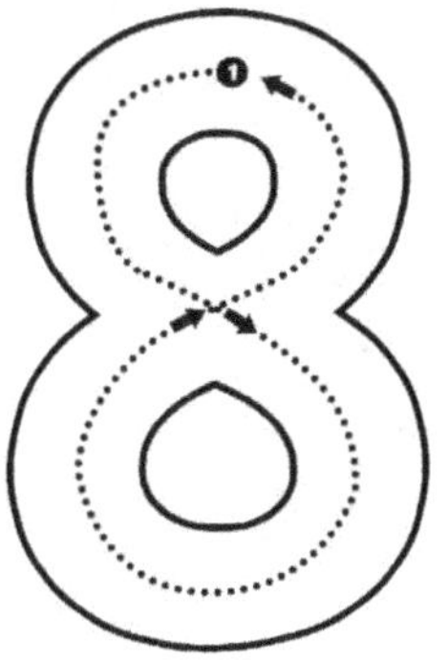

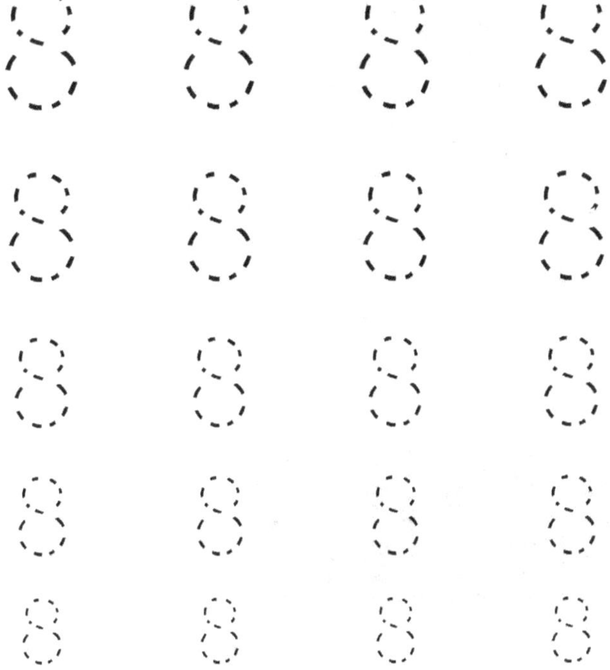

Count the Dots.

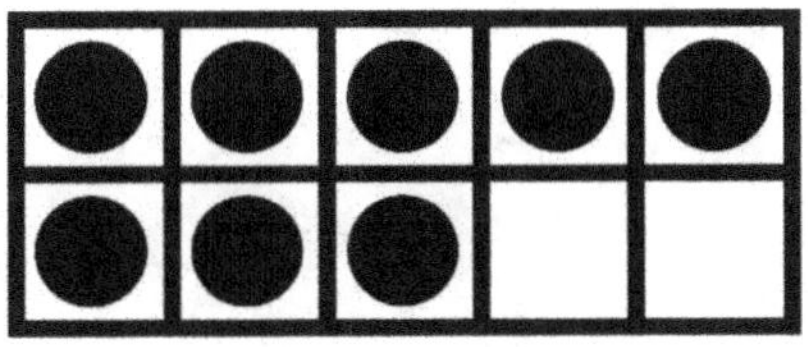

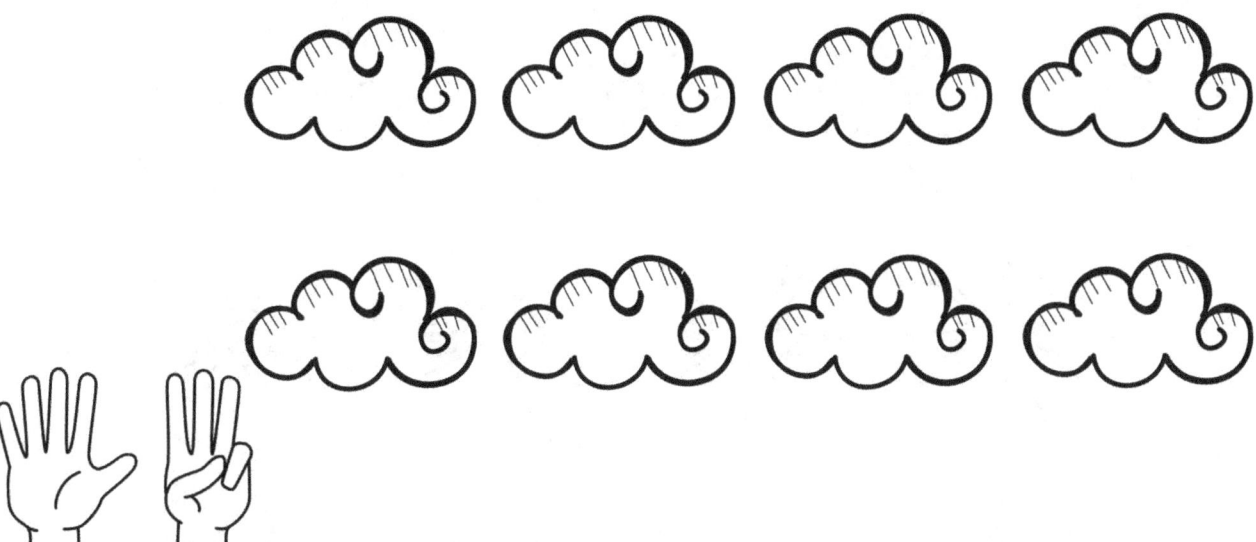

Look at the eight blue clouds in the sky!

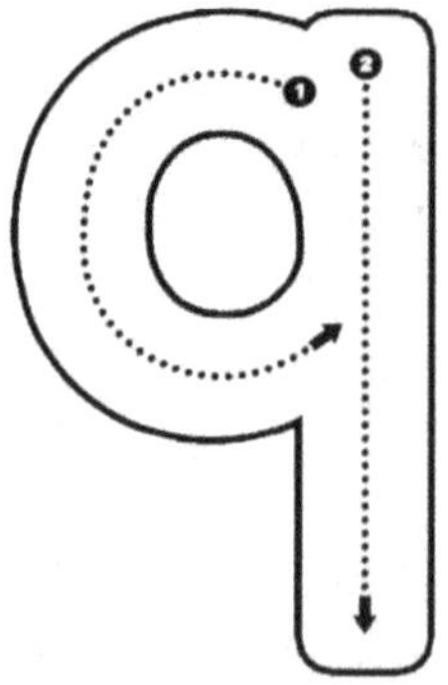

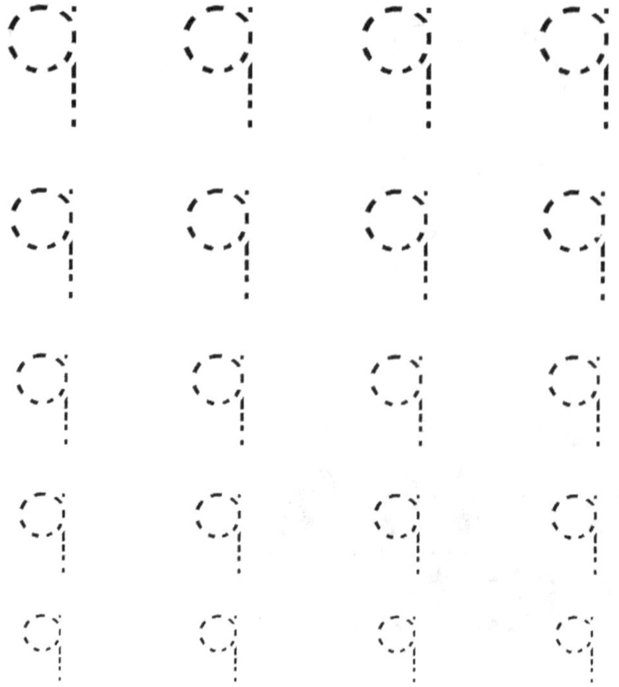

q

Count the Dots.

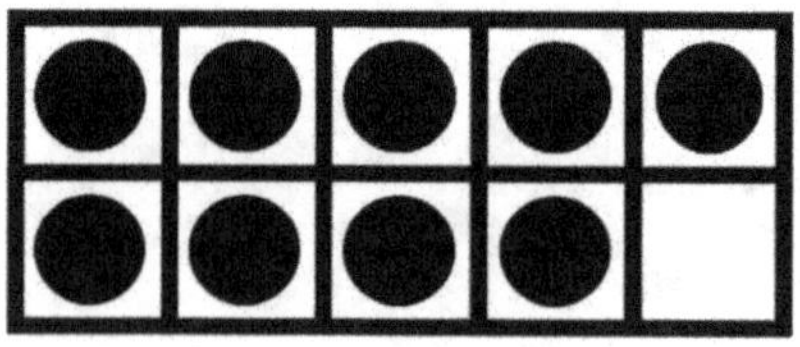

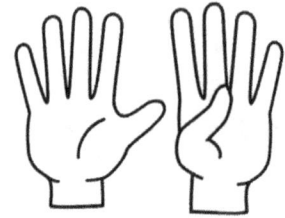

Color the nine shiny stars yellow.

10

Count the Dots.

Zaq gave ten green leaves to his mother.

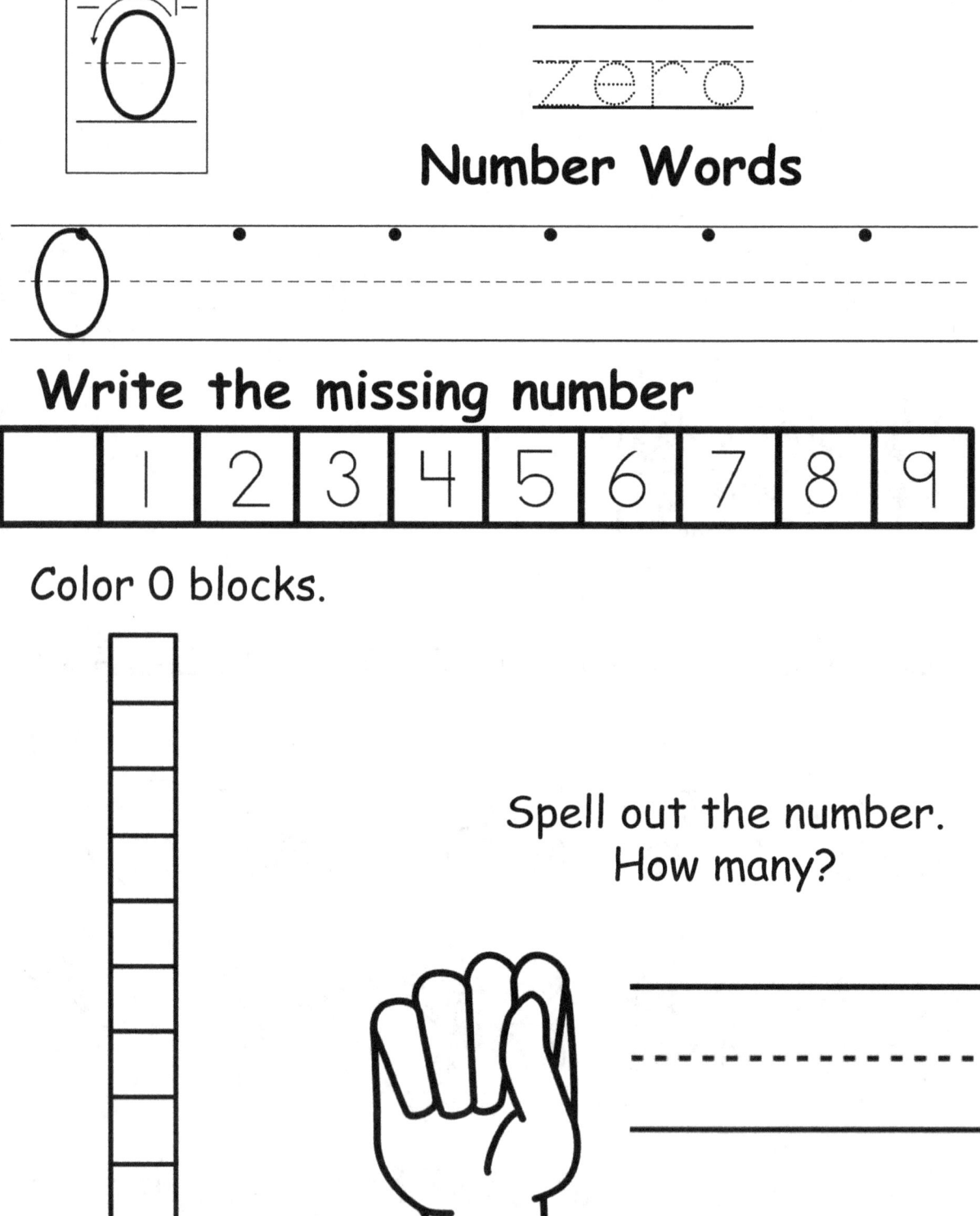

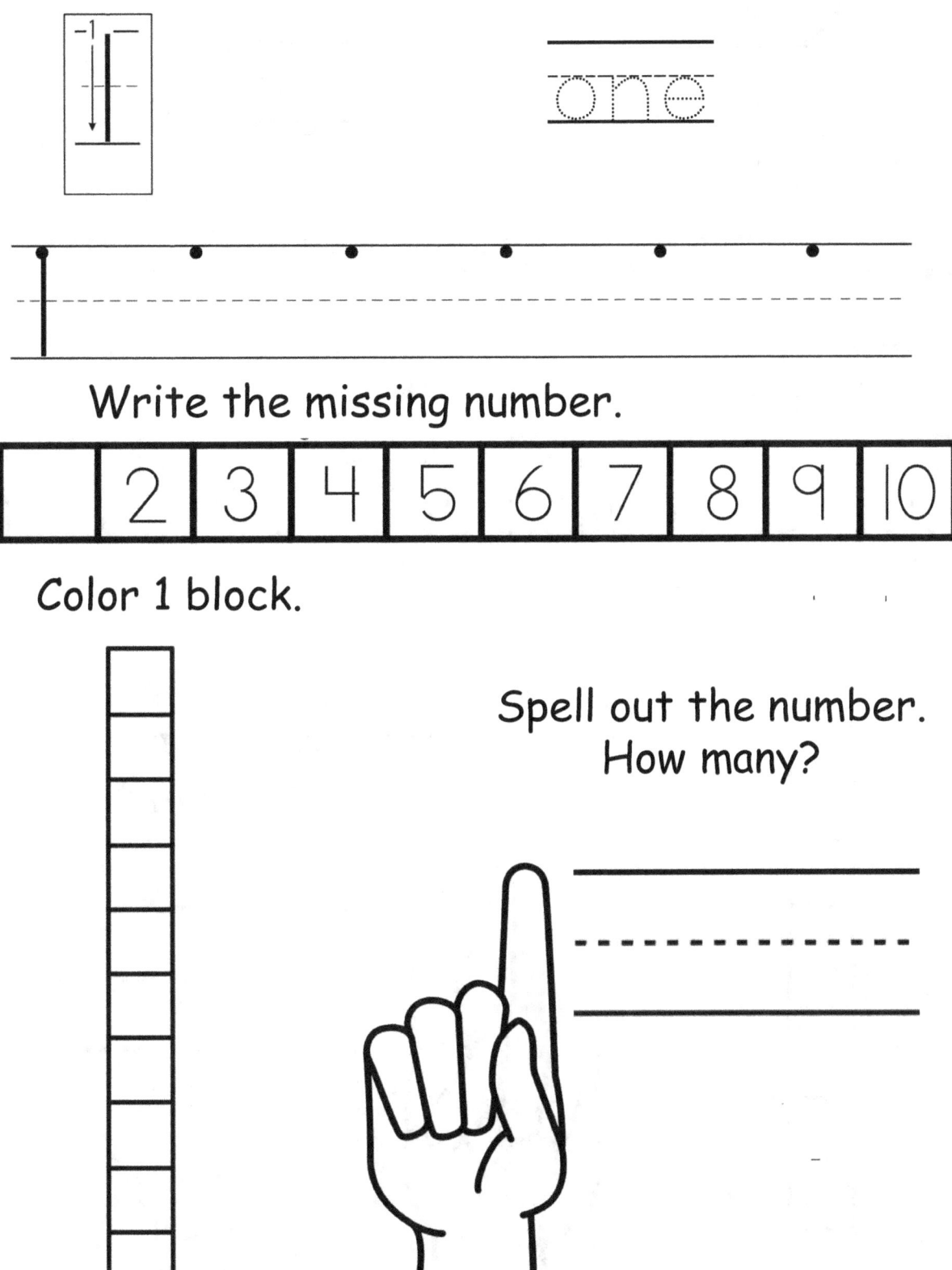

Write the missing number.

| 1 | | 3 | 4 | 5 | 6 | 7 | 8 | 9 | 10 |

Color 2 blocks.

Spell out the number. How many?

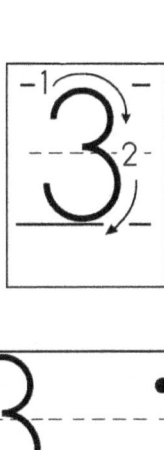 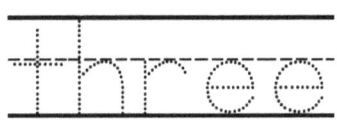

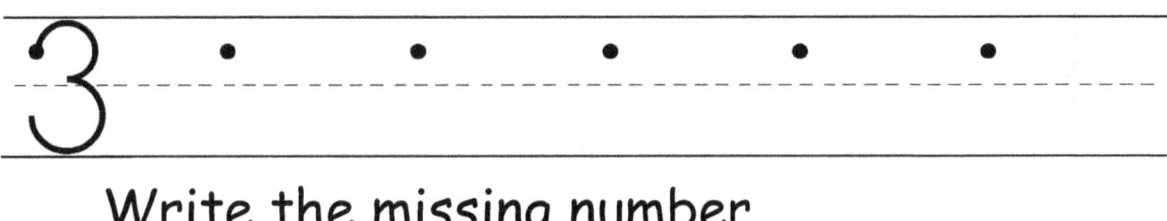

Write the missing number.

| 1 | 2 | | 4 | 5 | 6 | 7 | 8 | 9 | 10 |

Color 3 block.

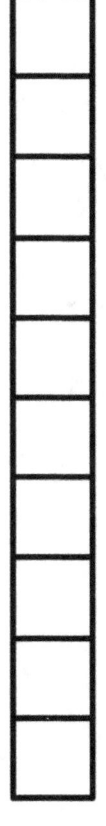

Spell out the number.
How many?

four

Write the missing number.

| 1 | 2 | 3 | | 5 | 6 | 7 | 8 | 9 | 10 |

Color 4 blocks.

Spell out the number.
How many?

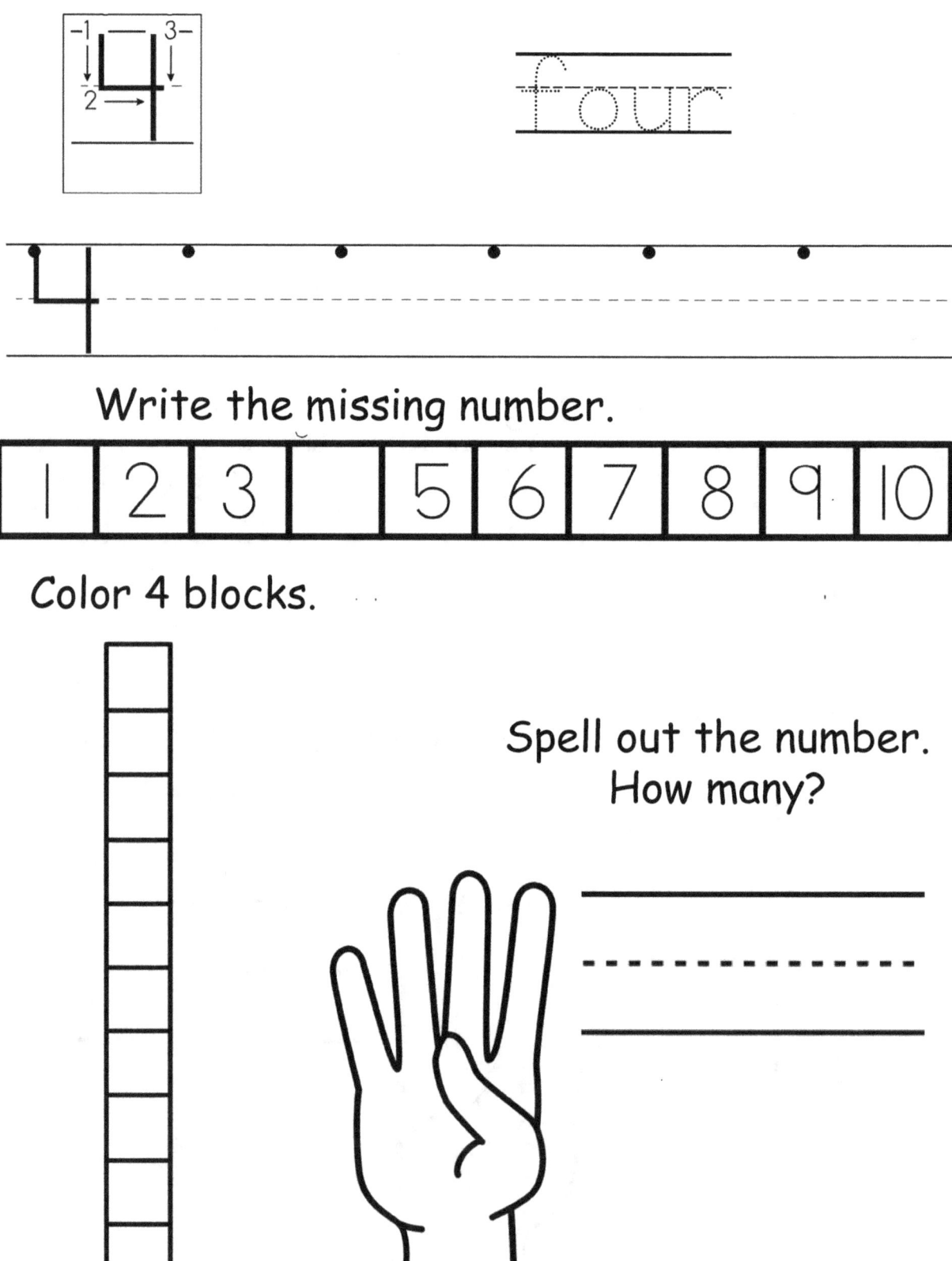

26

Write the missing number.

Color 5 block.

Spell out the number. How many?

6   six

Write the missing number.

| 1 | 2 | 3 | 4 | 5 | | 7 | 8 | 9 | 10 |

Color 6 blocks.

Spell out the number.
How many?

_____

- - - - - - - - - - - - - -

_____

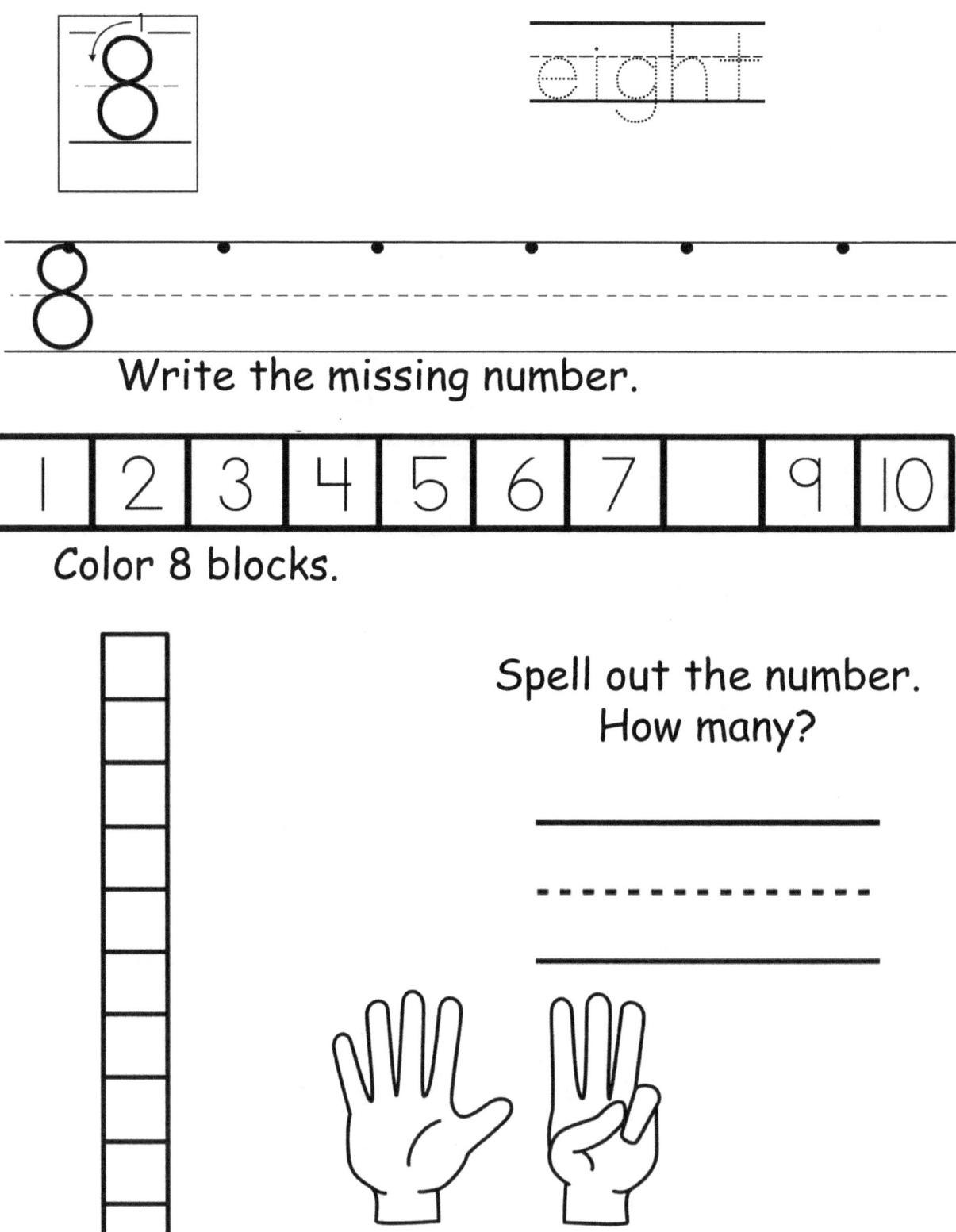

Write the missing number.

Color 8 blocks.

Spell out the number.
How many?

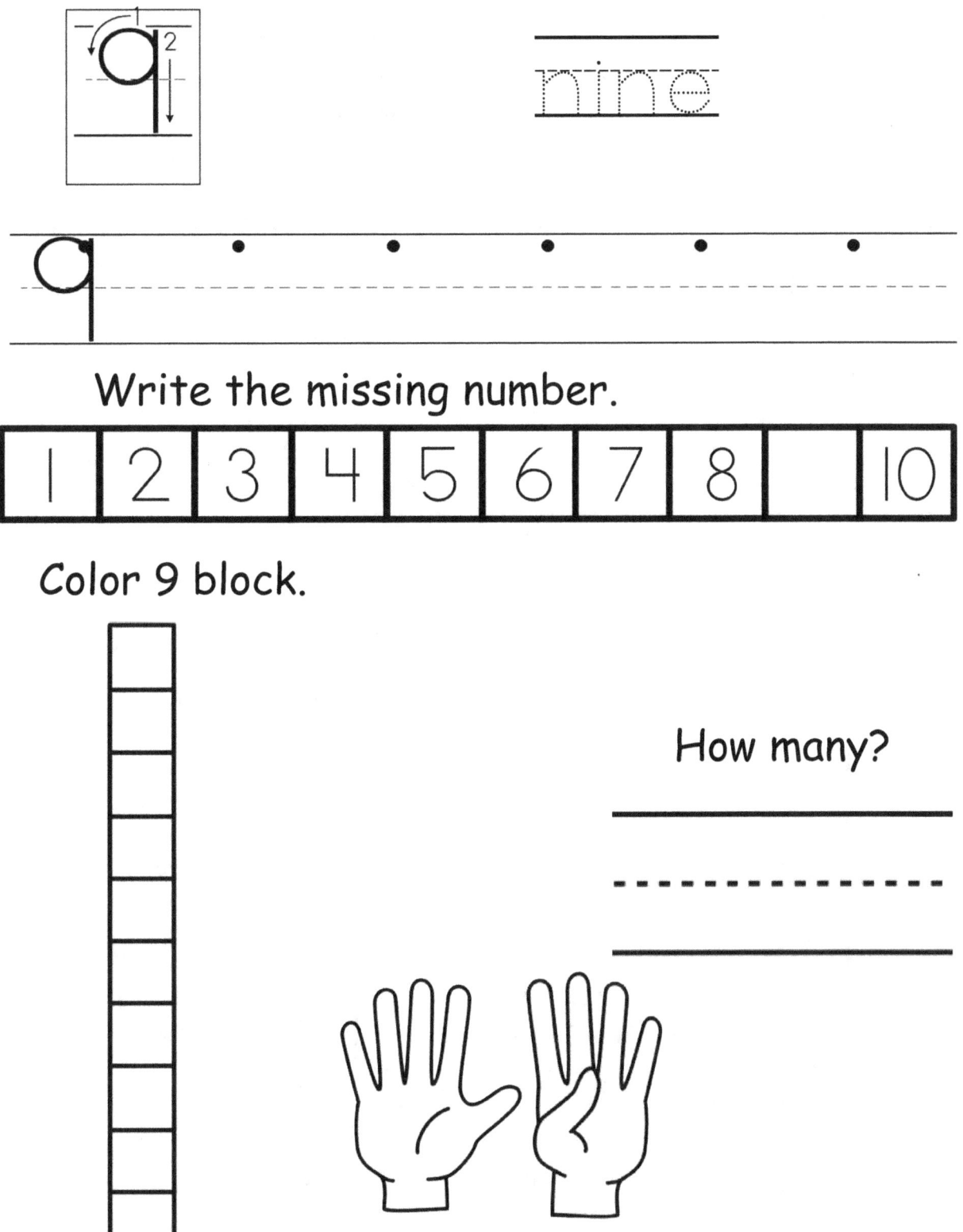

Write the missing number.

Color 9 block.

How many?

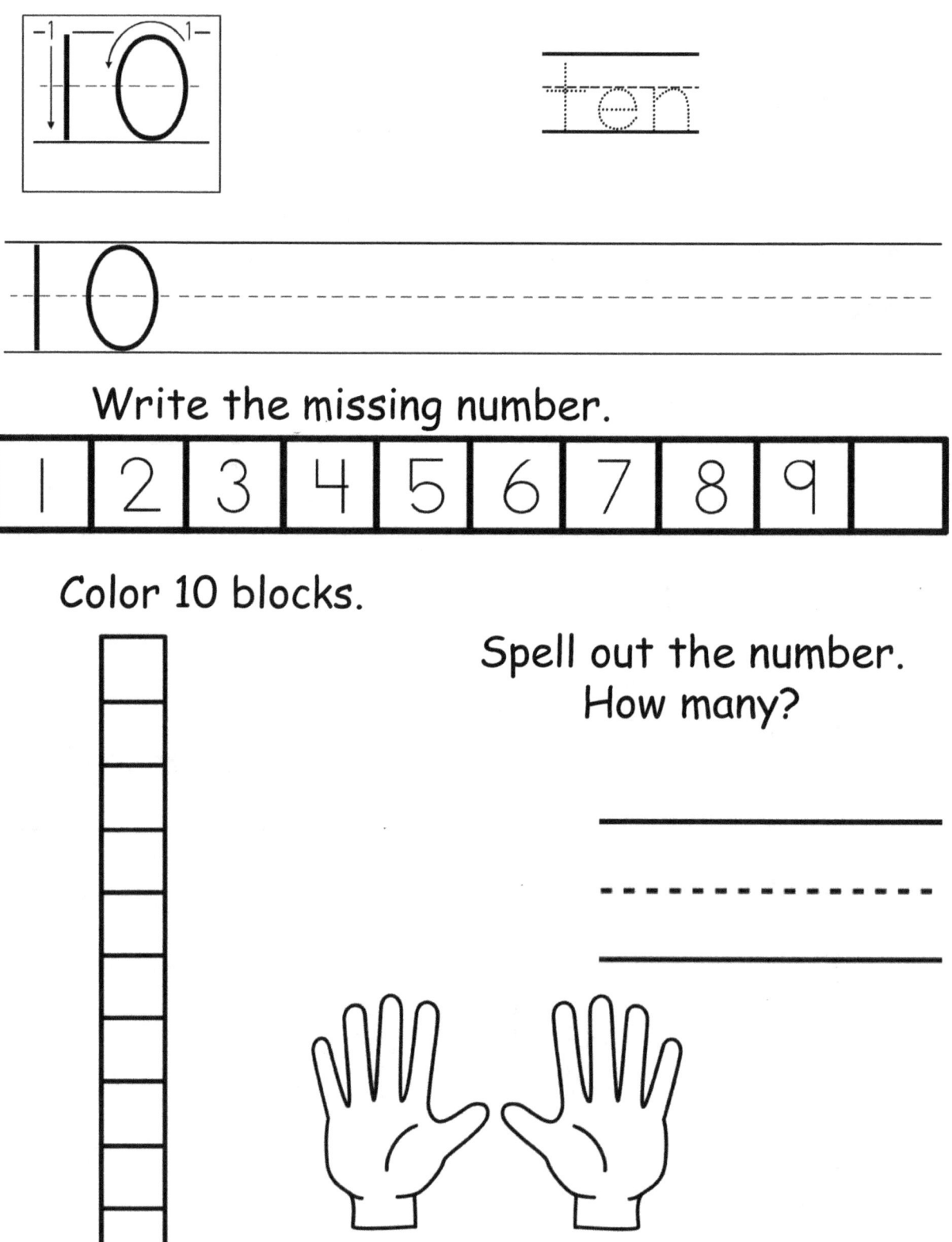

Write the missing number.

Color 10 blocks.

Spell out the number.
How many?

Number Words Match

Draw a line from the hands to the matching number words.

   five

   one

   four

   two

   three

Number Words

Draw a line from the hands to the matching number words.

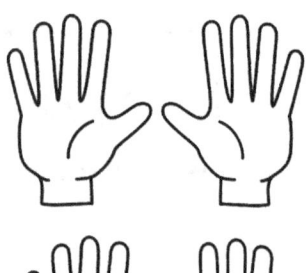

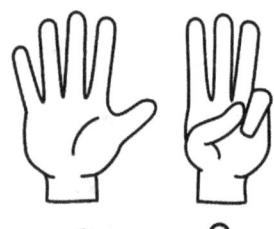

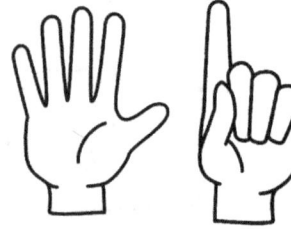

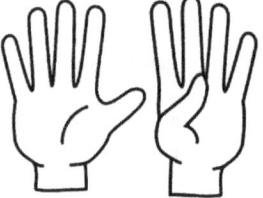

six

nine

ten

eight

seven

Trace the numbers and words. Then write numbers 1 to 10.

1	2	3	4	5
6	7	8	9	10

one two three
four five six
seven eight nine
ten

I Can Write to Twenty

1	2	3	4	5
6	7	8	9	10
11	12	13	14	15
16	17	18	19	20

eleven   twelve   thirteen
fourteen   fifteen   sixteen
seventeen   eighteen
nineteen   twenty

I Can Write to Thirty

1	2	3	4	5
6	7	8	9	10
11	12	13	14	15
16	17	18	19	20
21	22	23	24	25
26	27	28	29	30

twenty-one
twenty-two
twenty-three
twenty-four
twenty-five

Trace words and write numbers 21 to 30.

twenty-six
twenty-seven
twenty-eight
twenty-nine
thirty

I Can Write to Forty

1	2	3	4	5
6	7	8	9	10
11	12	13	14	15
16	17	18	19	20
21	22	23	24	25
26	27	28	29	30

| 31 | 32 | 33 | 34 | 35 |
| 36 | 37 | 38 | 39 | 40 |

Color the necklace your favorite colors.
Count the beads and write the number.

I Can Write to Fifty

1	2	3	4	5
6	7	8	9	10
11	12	13	14	15
16	17	18	19	20
21	22	23	24	25
26	27	28	29	30

31	32	33	34	35
36	37	38	39	40
41	42	43	44	45
46	47	48	49	50

Color your rabbit and give it a name.

Missing Numbers

Write the misssing numbers.

	2		4	
6		8		10
	12	13		15
16		18	19	

21		23		25
	27	28	29	
31			34	35
36	37		39	
	42	43		45
46		48	49	

Color your cupcake and drink.

44

I Can Count by 2s

2	4	6	8	10
12	14	16	18	20
22	24	26	28	30
32	34	36	38	40
42	44	46	48	50

Color your butterfly and give it a name.

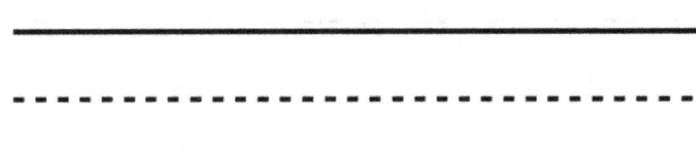

I Can Count by 5s

5	10	15	20	25
30	35	40	45	50
55	60	65	70	75
80	85	90	95	100

Color the bat.
Give it a name.

_____

_____

I Can Count by 10s

| 10 | 20 | 30 | 40 | 50 |
| 60 | 70 | 80 | 90 | 100 |

Ten   Sixty

Twenty   Seventy

Thirty   Eighty

Forty   Ninety

Fifty   One Hundred

1 - 100 Chart

1	2	3	4	5	6	7	8	9	10
11	12	13	14	15	16	17	18	19	20
21	22	23	24	25	26	27	28	29	30
31	32	33	34	35	36	37	38	39	40
41	42	43	44	45	46	47	48	49	50
51	52	53	54	55	56	57	58	59	60
61	62	63	64	65	66	67	68	69	70
71	72	73	74	75	76	77	78	79	80
81	82	83	84	85	86	87	88	89	90
91	92	93	94	95	96	97	98	99	100

No Peeking!
Write all numbers
1 to 100

Keep going!

Keep going!

Good Job!

Use your favorite colors to color Koko koloko.

Color and Count

How many?

54

Count, then circle the number to show how many.

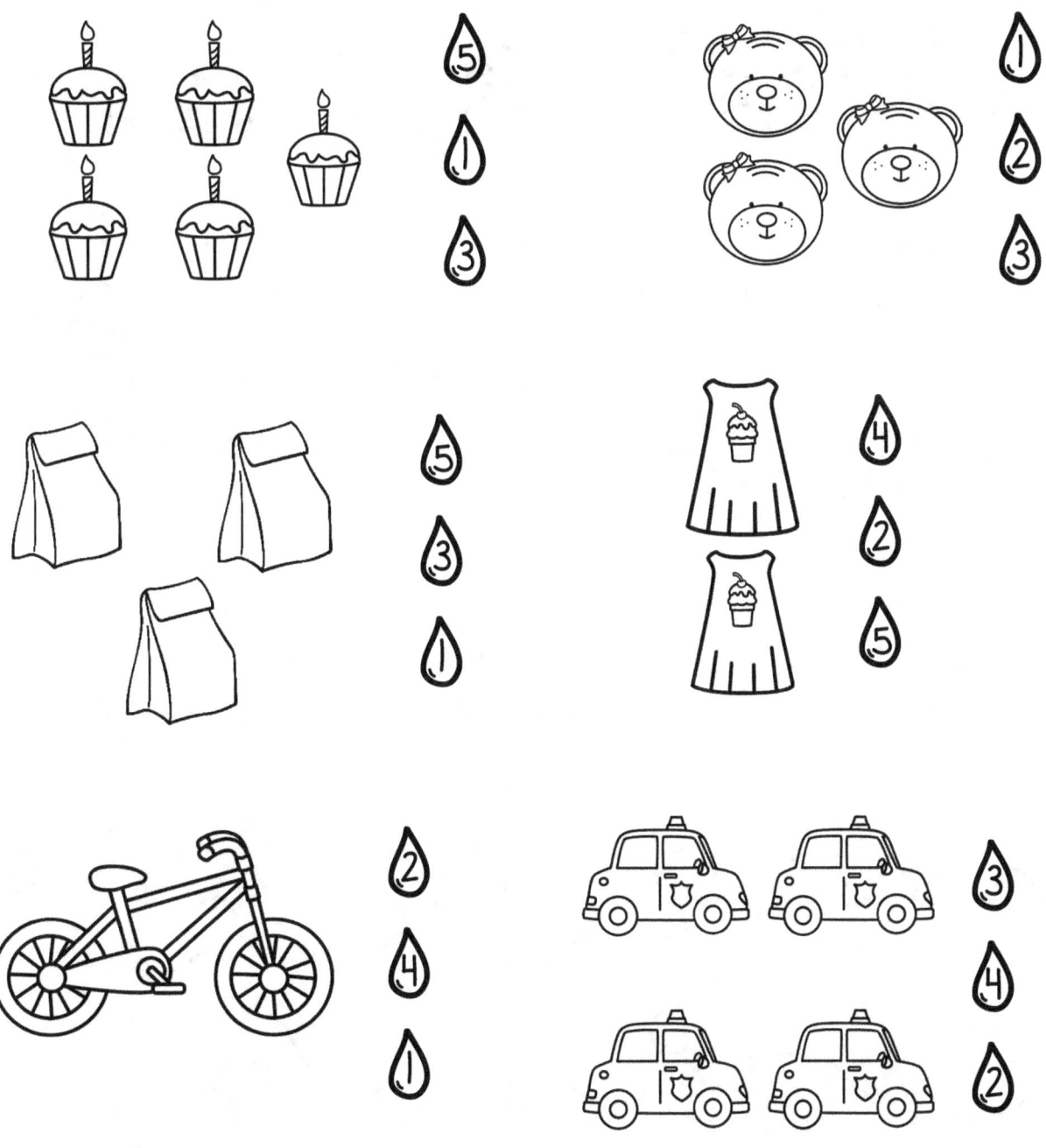

Count, then circle the number
to show how many.

Write numbers 1 to 10

What's the big deal?

Which Number is Larger?
Check the box.

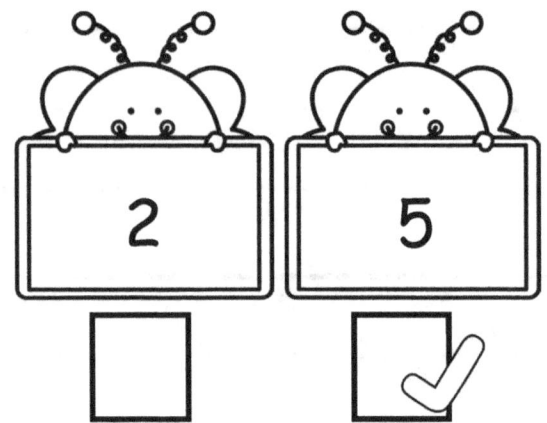

Spell the smaller number.

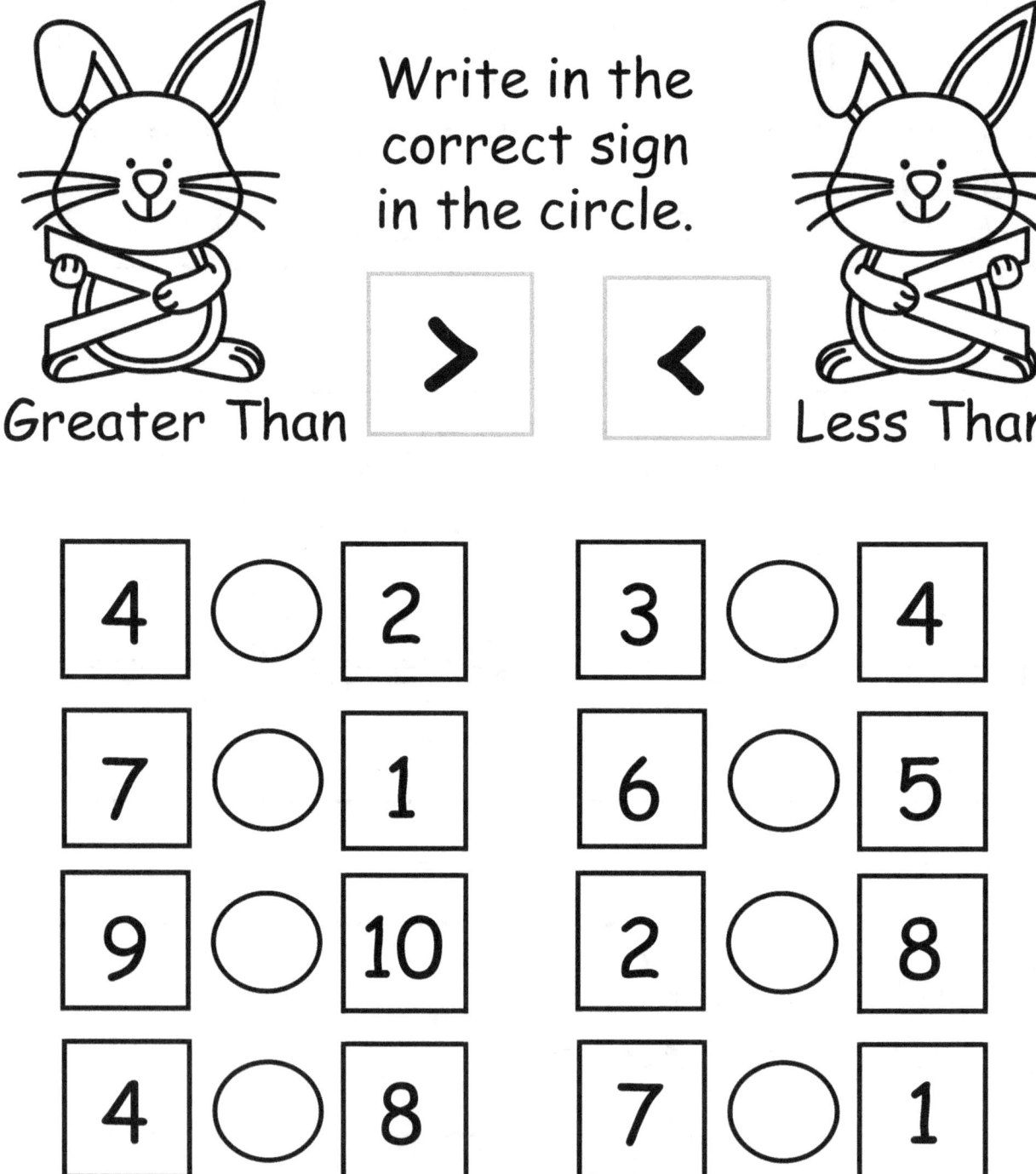

5 ◯ 8	9 ◯ 1
2 ◯ 0	3 ◯ 7
9 ◯ 6	5 ◯ 4
7 ◯ 4	8 ◯ 2

18 ◯ 13	15 ◯ 10
14 ◯ 16	11 ◯ 8
9 ◯ 17	13 ◯ 19
10 ◯ 20	12 ◯ 14

Addition Word List

total
altogether
join
both
How many in all?

sum
plus
combined
increase
together
add
plus

Gus the Plus... is a generous young man, giving to others whenever he can! He will show you how many you have in **all**, when he comes around your **sum** will grow tall! He **adds** numbers **together** so that you will have **more**, with help from Gus adding is never a chore!

5   1 = 6

ADDITION Strategies

My fingers

I can use my fingers to add numbers.

Color the fingers to show the equation:
3+4=7

Snap cubes

I can use snap cubes to add numbers.

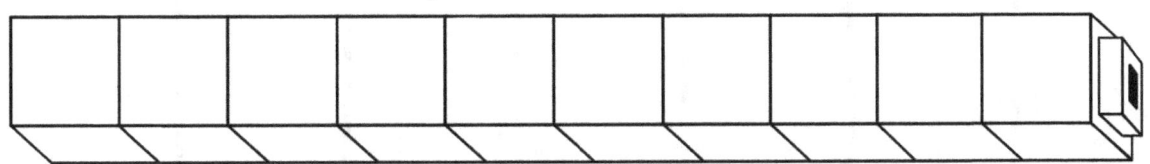

Use 2 colors to show the equation:
4+6=10

Number Line

I can use a number line to add numbers.

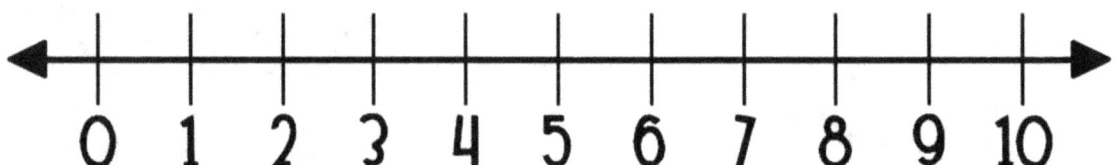

Use the number line to show the equation:
5+5=10

Ten frames

I can use ten frames to add numbers.

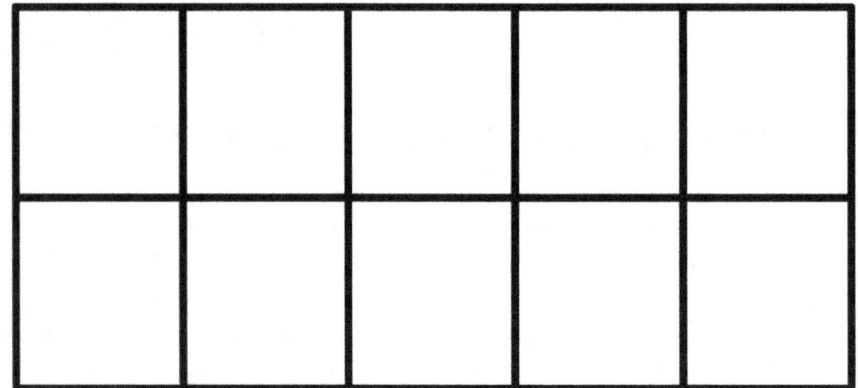

Use the ten frame to show the equation:
7+3=10

Counters

I can use counters to add numbers; like rocks, marbles, or sticks.

Draw pictures of your counters to show the equation: **1+9=10**

Count the Dots
Write the number below.

Draw Pictures

I can draw pictures of dots to add numbers.

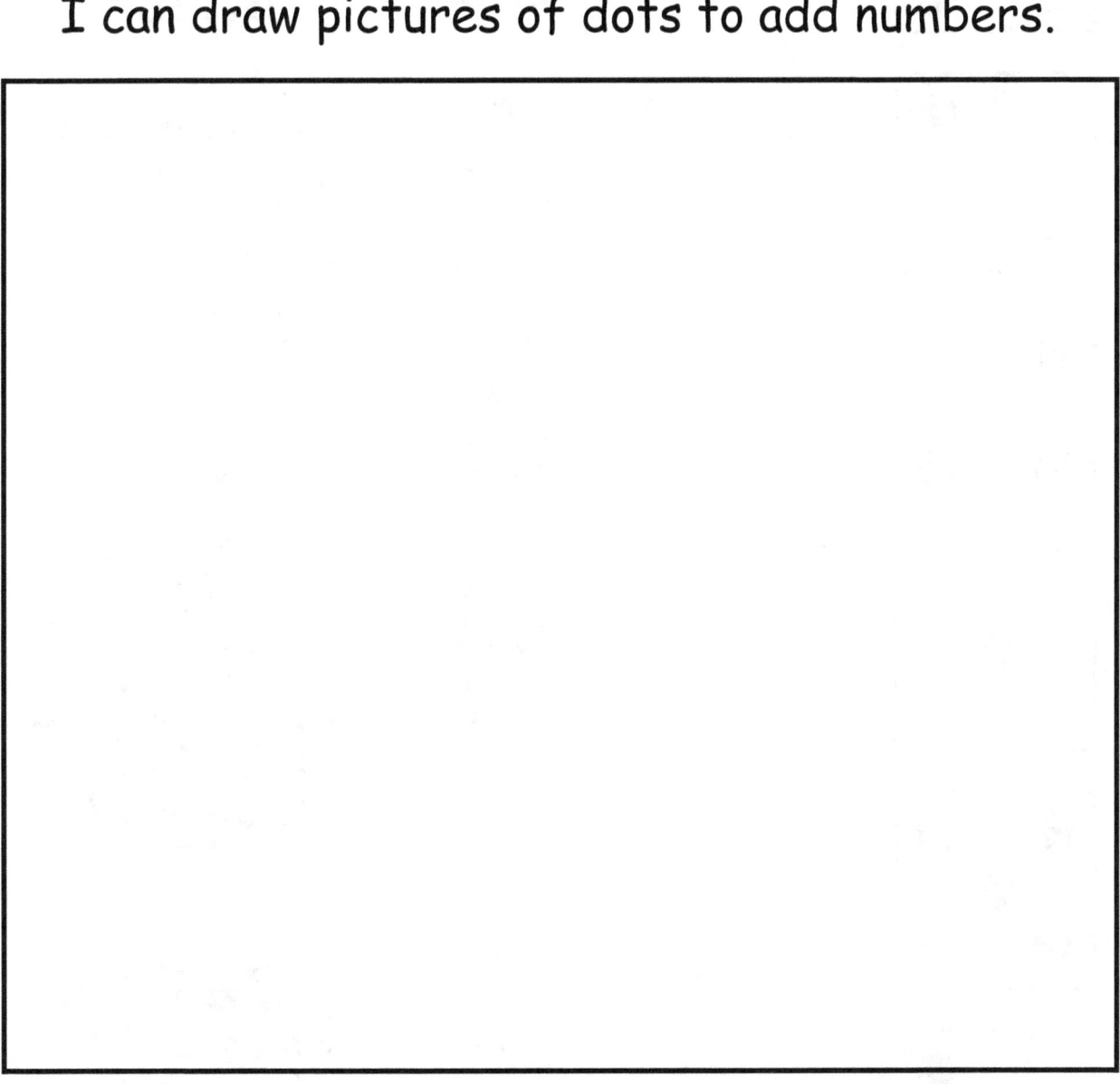

Draw picture to show the equation:
1+9=10

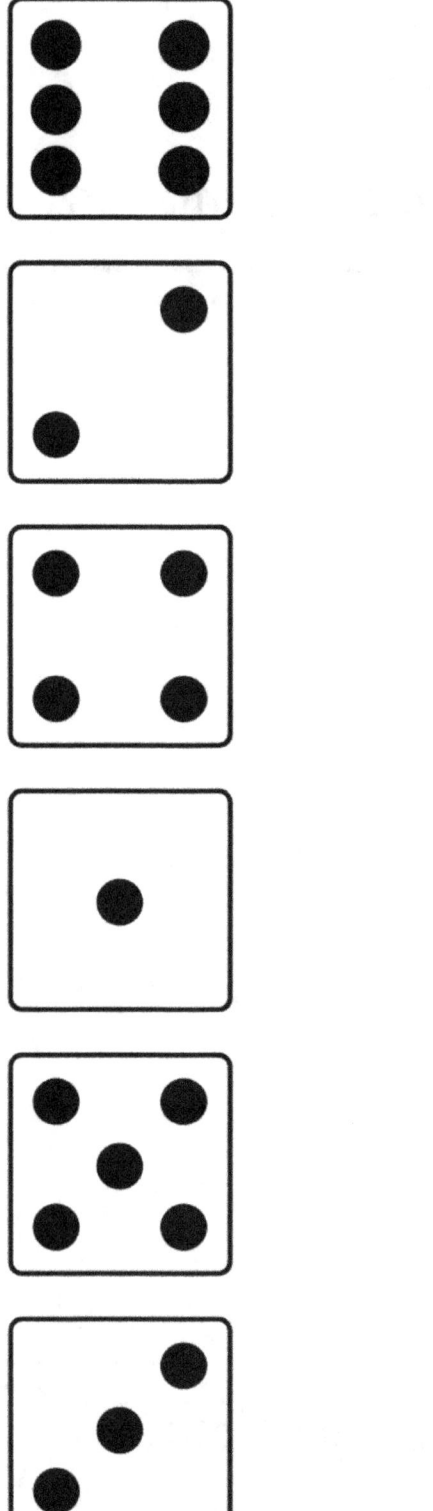

Count and Match

Draw a line to match the number and picture.

Domino Addition

Count the number of dots on each domino and write the numbers on the lines. Add up the dots and put the sum in the box.

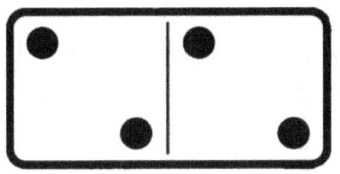   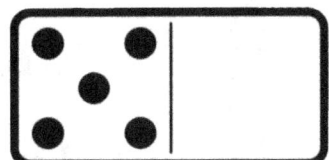

___ + ___ = ☐   ___ + ___ = ☐

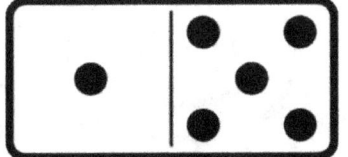

___ + ___ = ☐   ___ + ___ = ☐

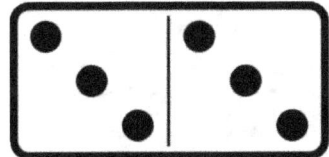

___ + ___ = ☐   ___ + ___ = ☐

sum
plus
combined
increase
together
add
plus

total
altogether
join
both

How many in all?

Addition

Add   +

1 + 1 = 2

3 + 1 = 4

4 + 1 = 5

0 + 1 = 1

1 + 1 = 2

2 + 3 = 5

4 + 2 = 6

3 + 1 = 4

Solve the Problems

1 + 1 = _____   1 + 5 = _____

1 + 2 = _____   1 + 6 = _____

1 + 3 = _____   1 + 7 = _____

1 + 4 = _____   1 + 8 = _____

2 + 2 = _____

2 + 3 = _____

2 + 4 = _____

2 + 5 = _____

5 + 1 = ─────
6 + 2 = ─────
7 + 3 = ─────
1 + 2 = ─────

3 + 2 = ─────   1 + 7 = ─────
3 + 3 = ─────   0 + 3 = ─────
3 + 4 = ─────   2 + 4 = ─────
3 + 5 = ─────   2 + 0 = ─────
4 + 1 = ─────   3 + 1 = ─────

3 + 7 =

9 + 2 =

4 + 5 =

5 + 3 =   1 + 8 =

6 + 4 =   0 + 7 =

8 + 2 =   1 + 5 =

5 + 5 =   6 + 6 =

6 + 3 =   2 + 7 =

0 + 8 =   1 + 4 =

Missing Numbers

Write the missing number in each problem.

0 + _____ = 1

3 + _____ = 7

2 + _____ = 5

3 + _____ = 4

1 + _____ = 5

2 + _____ = 2

1 + _____ = 3

0 + _____ = 4

2 + _____ = 3

4 + _____ = 5

More missing numbers to solve.

2 + _____ = 6

4 + _____ = 10

1 + _____ = 9

5 + _____ = 7

Tell the Truth

2 + 1 = 4

True   False
☐   ☐

Solve the equations to tell if they are true or false.

0 + 5 = 5

True   False
☐   ☐

2 + 2 = 4

True   False
☐   ☐

3 + 1 = 2

True   False
☐   ☐

1 + 4 = 5

True   False
☐   ☐

1 + 1 = 2

True   False
☐   ☐

Tell the Truth

Solve the equations to tell if they are true or false.

0 + 1 = 0

True False
☐   ☐

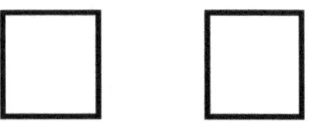

6 + 1 = 5

True False
☐   ☐

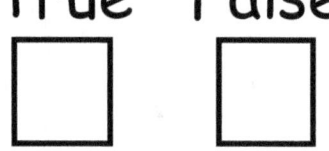

4 + 1 = 3

True False
☐   ☐

3 + 3 = 6

True False
☐   ☐

8 + 1 = 9

True False
☐   ☐

2 + 5 = 7

True False
☐   ☐

Fishing for Equations

Addition

Use the numbers inside each fish to write 3 addition equations.

___ + ___ = ___   ___ + ___ = ___

___ + ___ = ___   ___ + ___ = ___

___ + ___ = ___   ___ + ___ = ___

 Solve the equations.

2 + 3 = ___

0 + 4 = ___

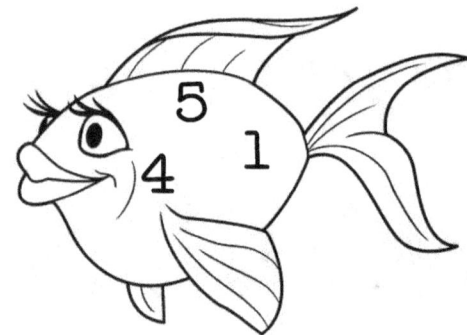 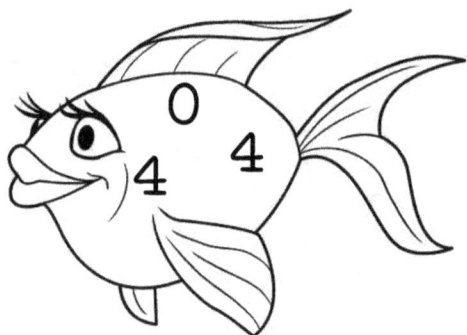

___ + ___ = ___   ___ + ___ = ___

___ + ___ = ___   ___ + ___ = ___

___ + ___ = ___   ___ + ___ = ___

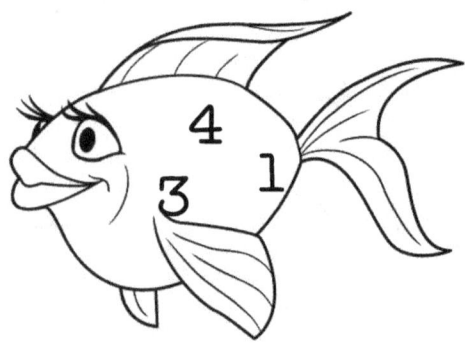 

___ + ___ = ___   ___ + ___ = ___

___ + ___ = ___   ___ + ___ = ___

___ + ___ = ___   ___ + ___ = ___

Seeing Double

Write each sum to its doubles fact.

 4

___ + ___ = ___

 6

___ + ___ = ___

2

___ + ___ = ___

 10

___ + ___ = ___

8

___ + ___ = ___

1 + 1
2 + 2
3 + 3
4 + 4
5 + 5

Subtraction Word List

How many more?
decrease
less than
take away
minus
difference
left
remains
"er" words; fewer, shorter, faster, longer, etc
subtract
How much more?

Linus the Minus... is a naughty rabbit, always **taking away**. He is oh so bad! When he comes around you will end up with **less**! He makes a big **difference**, but he will never confess!

How many more?

How much more?

decrease
less than
take away
minus
difference
left
remains
"er" words;
fewer
shorter
faster
longer

Subtraction Action

Take Away —

Cross out objects to show subtraction.

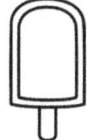   

4 - 4 = ___

4 - 1 = ___

Write the difference on the line.

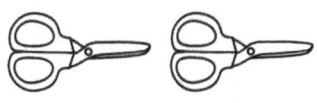

2 - 2 = ___

3 - 1 = ___

Cross out objects to show subtraction.

Write the difference on the line.

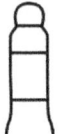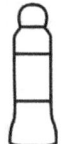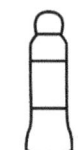

3 - 0 = ___

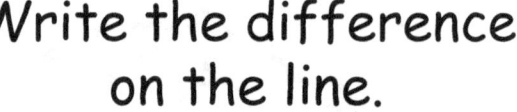

2 - 0 = ___

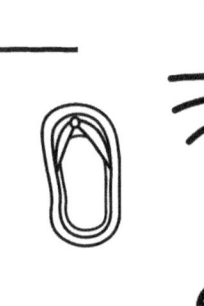

3 - 2 = ___

3 - 3 = ___

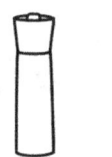 (5 clothespins)

2 - 1 = ___

5 - 4 = ___

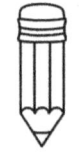 (4 pencils)

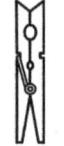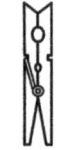

4 - 0 = ___

4 - 3 = ___

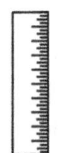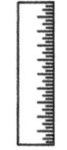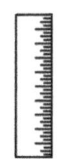

5 - 2 = ___

86

Subtraction Facts

Count the fingers and use them to help you solve the problems.

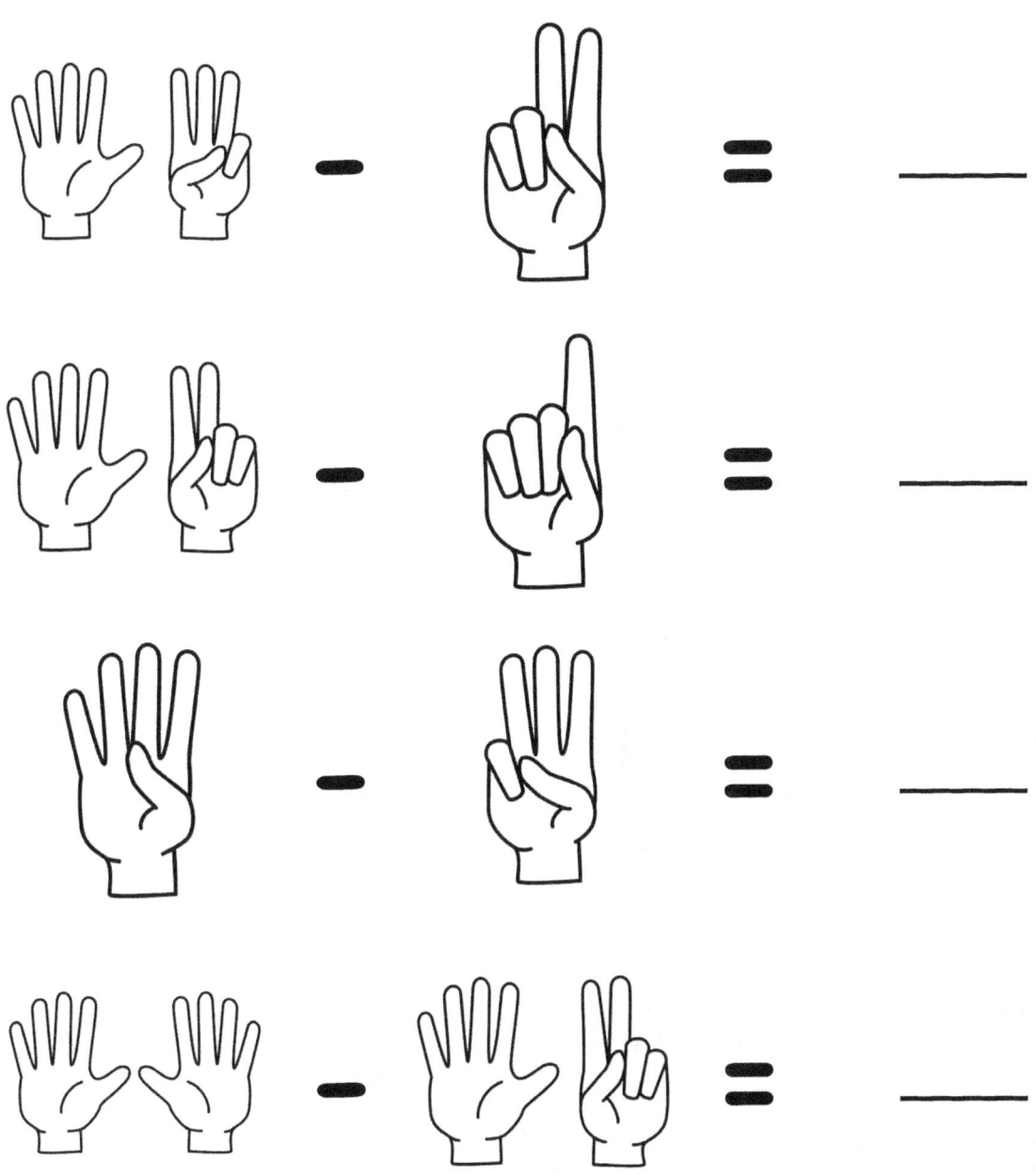

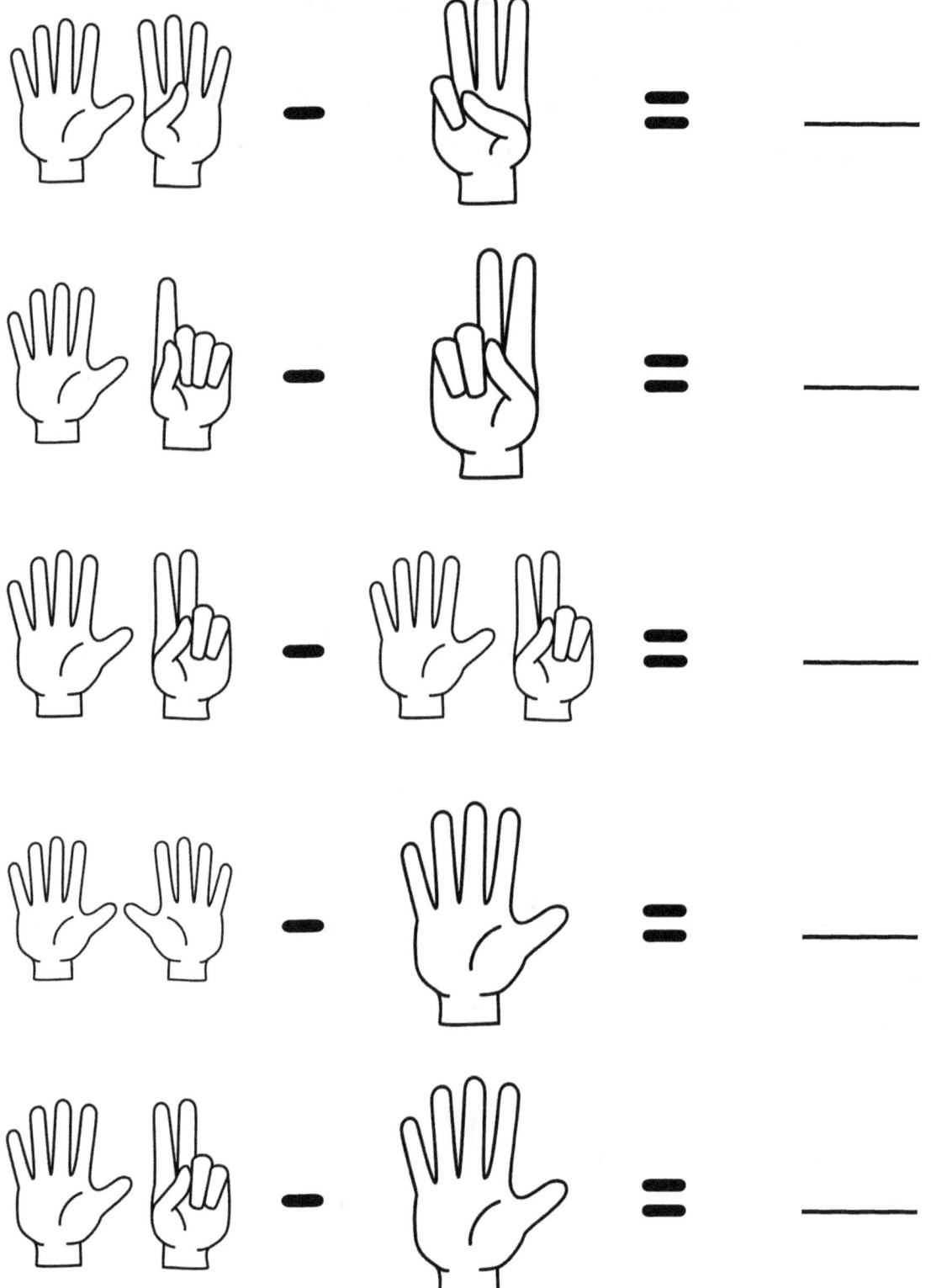

Draw a line from the problem to the matching hands to solve the problem.

8 - 3 =

5 - 4 =

4 - 2 =

8 - 8 =

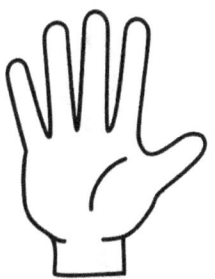

9 - 5 =

10 - 7 =

Circle the problem that does not belong.

Subtraction
Take Away

ten
10

10 - 2 = ☐

10 - 4 = ☐

10 - 6 = ☐

10 - 8 = ☐

10 - 10 = ☐

9 - 3 = ☐

5 - 1 = ☐

5 - 2 = ☐

5 - 3 = ☐

5 - 4 = ☐

5 - 5 = ☐

9 - 6 = ☐

9 - 9 = ☐

Shapes

circle	triangle	square

0 sides	3 sides	4 sides
0 vertices	3 vertices	4 vertices
		(all the same)

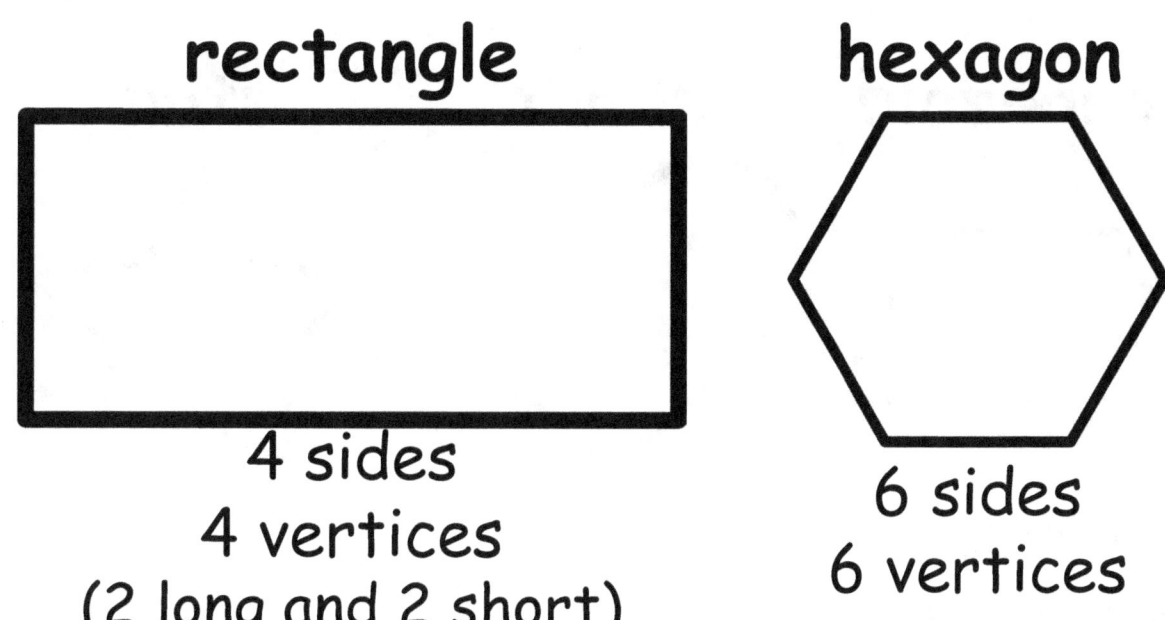

rectangle
4 sides
4 vertices
(2 long and 2 short)

hexagon
6 sides
6 vertices

The corners of the shapes are called, "vertices".

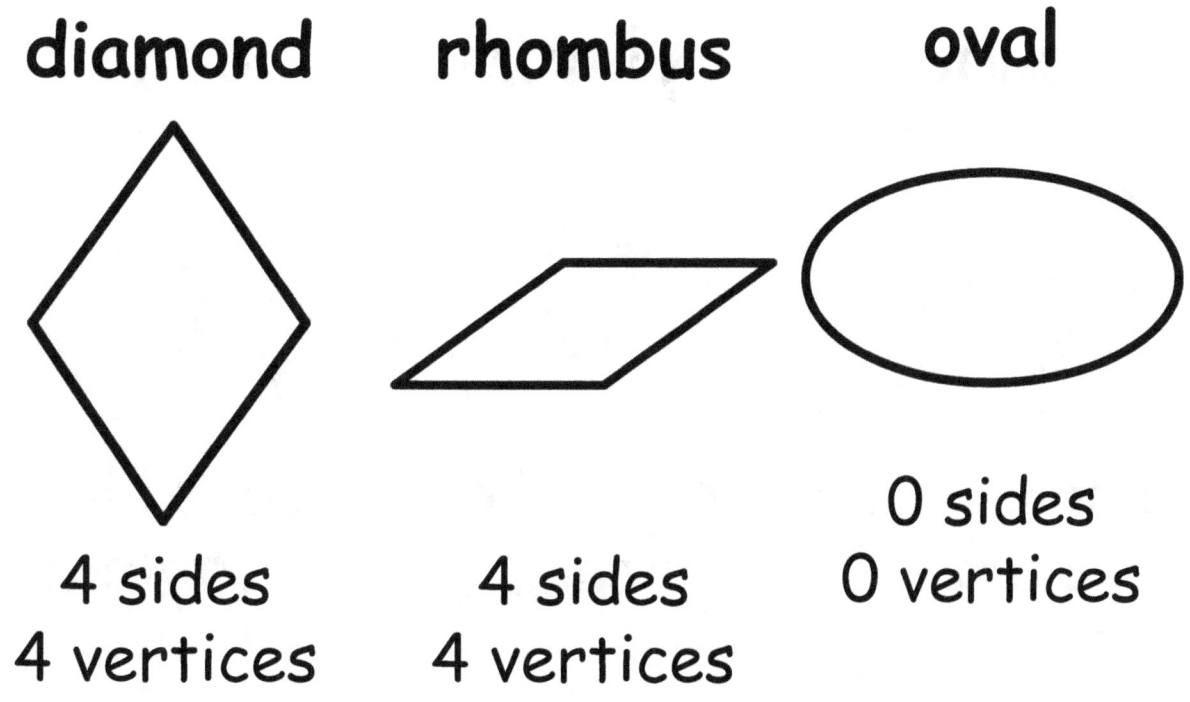

diamond
4 sides
4 vertices

rhombus
4 sides
4 vertices

oval
0 sides
0 vertices

trapezoid — heart — star

4 sides
4 vertices

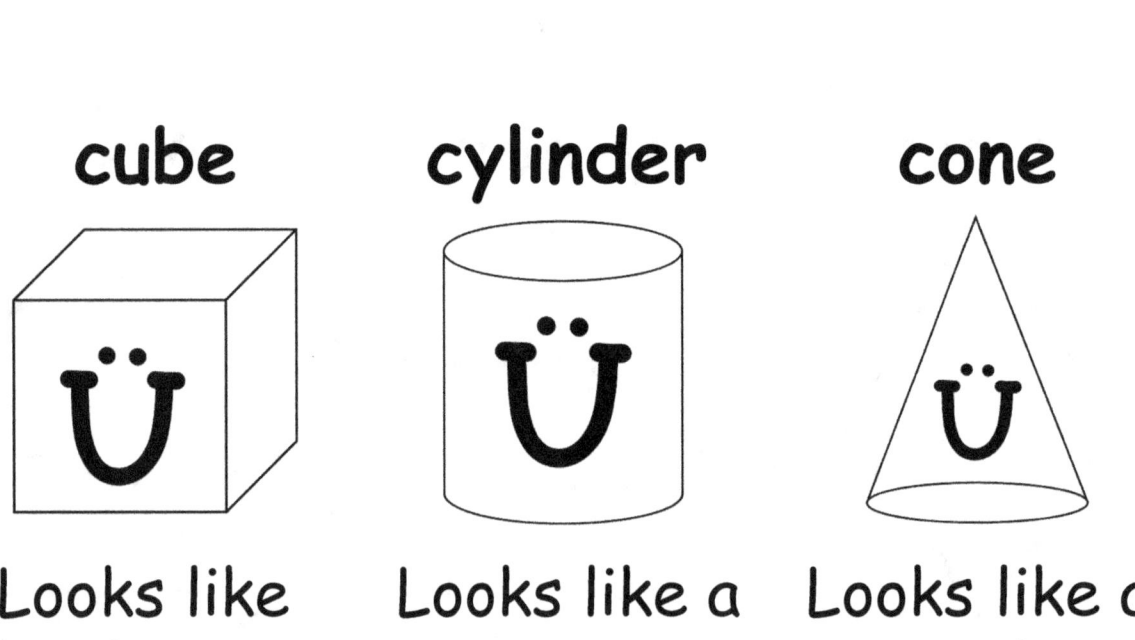

cube — cylinder — cone

Looks like a box.   Looks like a can.   Looks like a party hat.

sphere

Looks like a ball.

pyramid

Looks like a pyramid of Egypt.

rhombus

hexagon

star

Sides

3 = red
4 = yellow
5 = green
6 = orange
8 = blue

Color by Sides

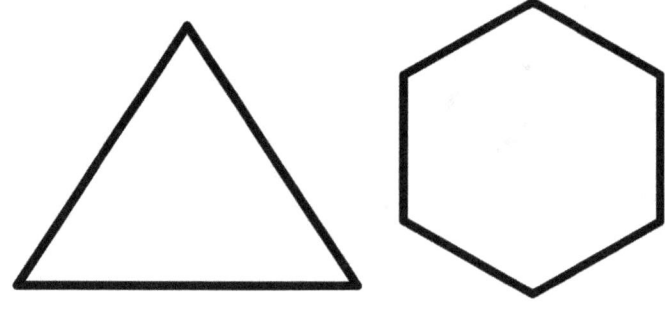
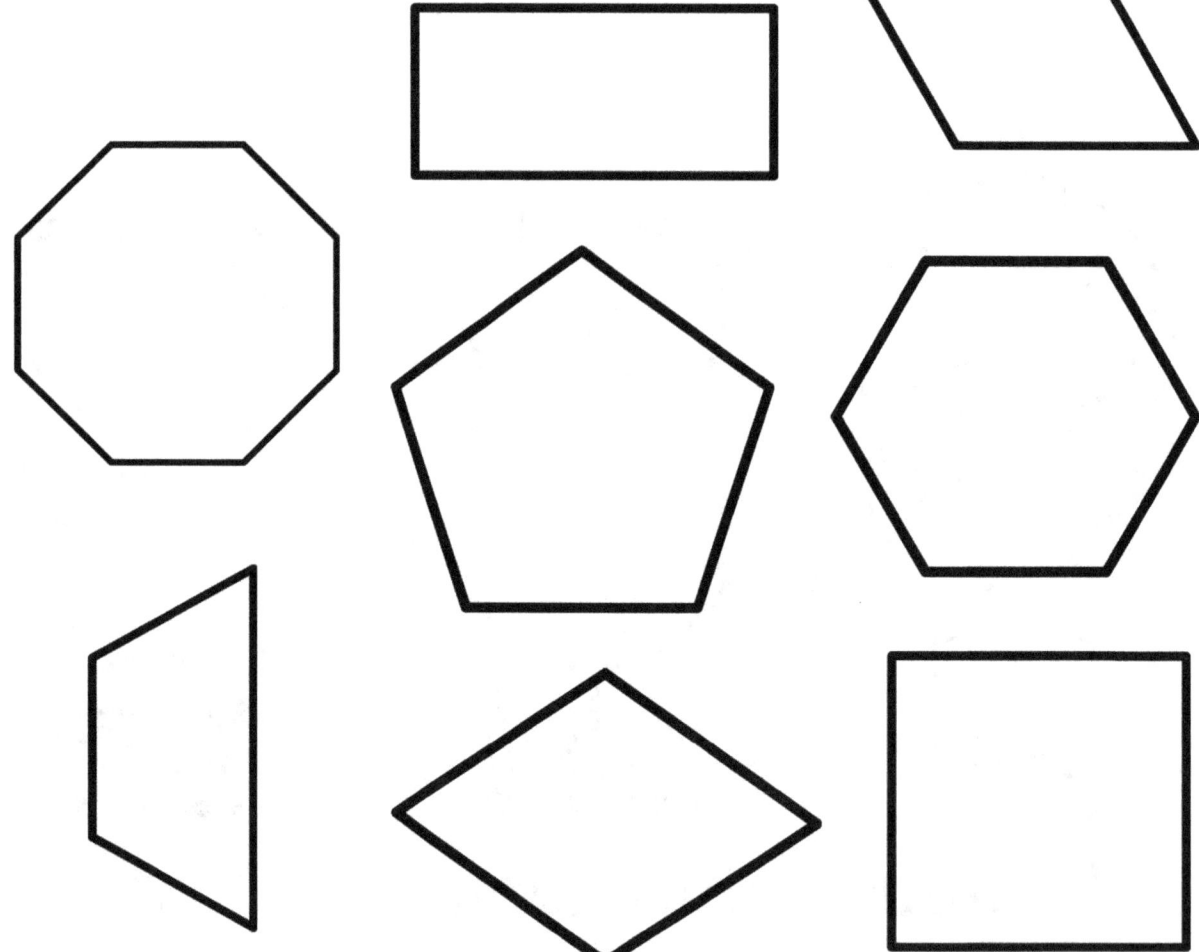

Sides

circle = red
oval = yellow
diamond = green
star = orange
heart = pink
crest = blue

Color by Shape

Shape Sort

Name of Shape	Draw Shape	Number of Sides	Number of Vertices
Circle	◯	0	0

Name of Shape	Draw Shape	Number of Sides	Number of Vertices

2D and 3D Shapes

2D

3D

100

Everyday 3D Shapes

Everyday 3D Shapes

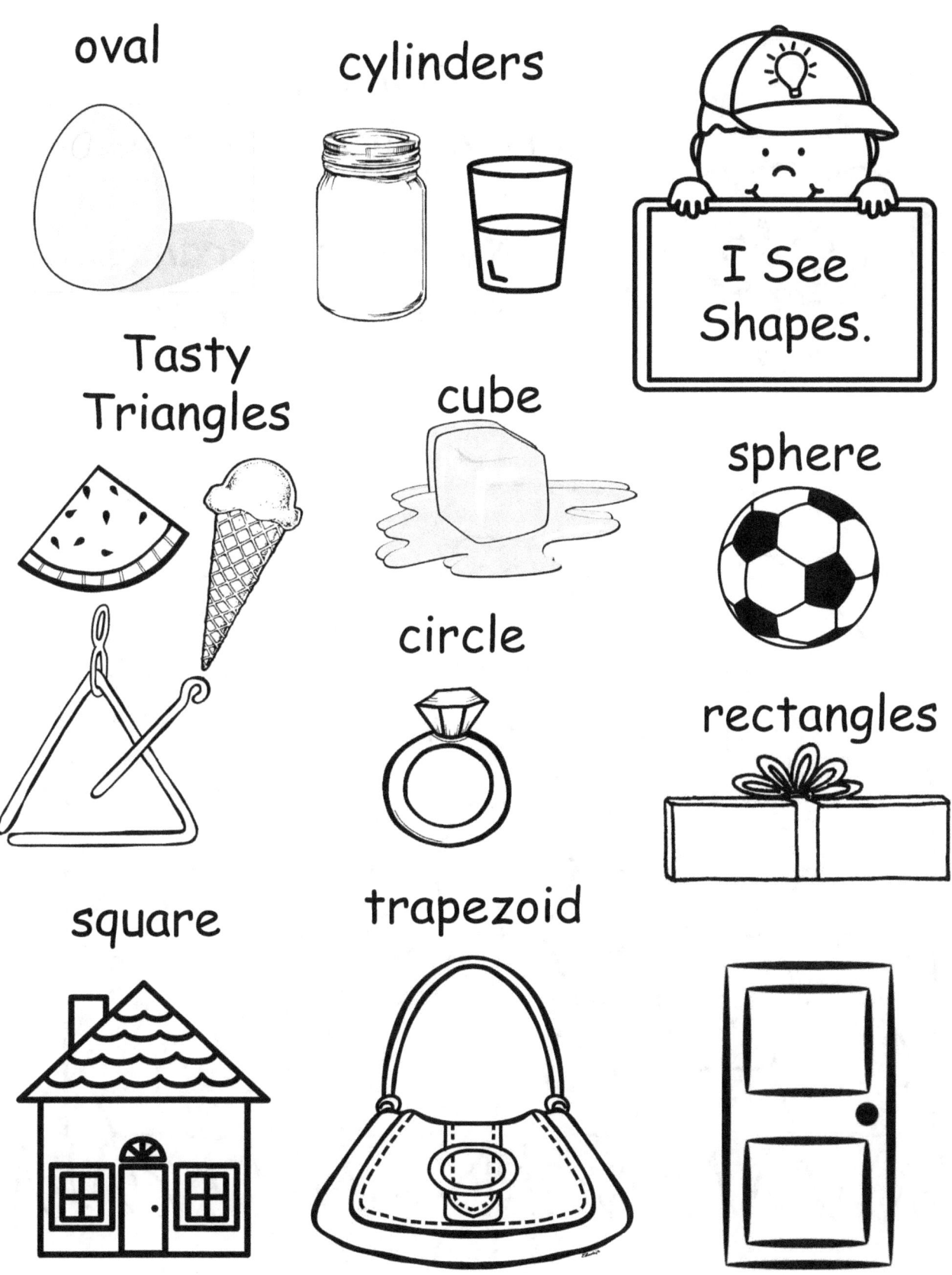

Color the Honeycomb Hexagons

1 - yellow 3 - orange
2 - green   4 - purple

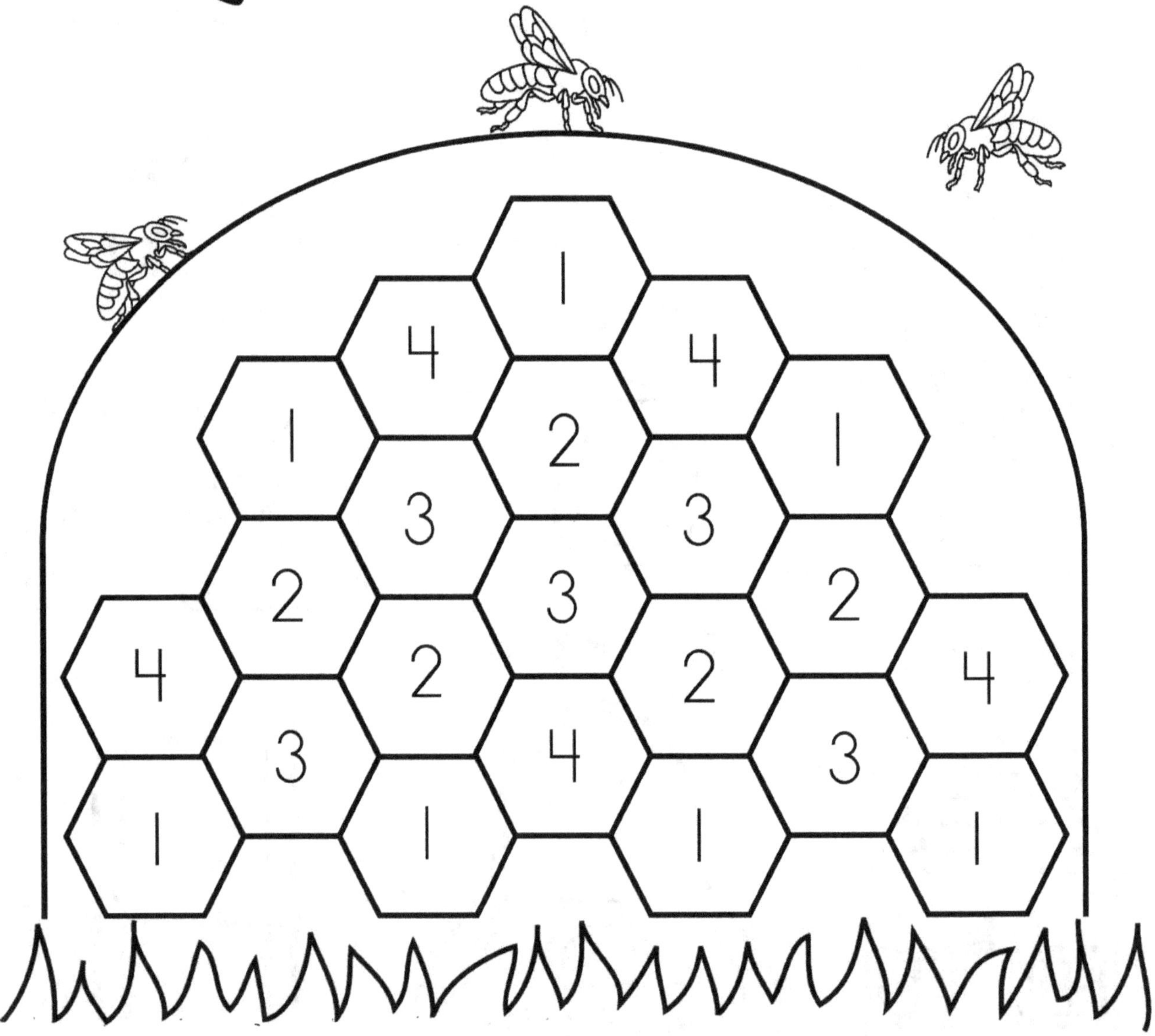

Order

What comes first; what comes next!

To put into a particular way.

Number Order		Place of position order	
1	6	first	sixth
2	7	second	seventh
3	8	third	eighth
4	9	fouth	nineth
5	10	fifth	tenth

Ordinal Numbers

Draw a line to match the numbers on the left to the words on the right.

	fifth
4th	seventh
1st	sixth
9th	
7th	first
2nd	fouth
6th	ninth
3rd	
10th	second
8th	eight
5th	third
	tenth

Passage of Time Order

yesterday

today

tomorrow

Daily events occur

morning

afternoon

night

Weekdays in order.

Sunday

Monday

Tuesday

Wednesday

Thursday

Friday

Saturday

Months in order.

January
February
March
April
May
June
July
August
September
October
November
December

Days of the Week
Which day comes next?

Days of the Week
Yesterday and Tomorrow

yesterday	today	tomorrow
	Wednesday	
	Monday	
	Tuesday	
	Thursday	
	Sunday	
	Friday	
	Saturday	

Place Preposition

in

on

under

between

Place Preposition

in

above

on

Musu is **beside** Zaq.

Occupying Space

Musu is **above** the tag.

Zaq is **below** the tag.

Zaq is **outside** the box.

Musu is **inside** the box.

Musu is **behind**.

Musu is **in front**.

 # Left and Right Position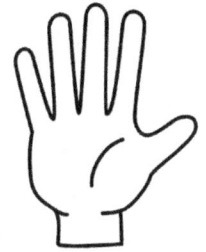

Which is left and which is right?

Circle the left fly

Circle the right chips

Circle the left bug

Circle the right key

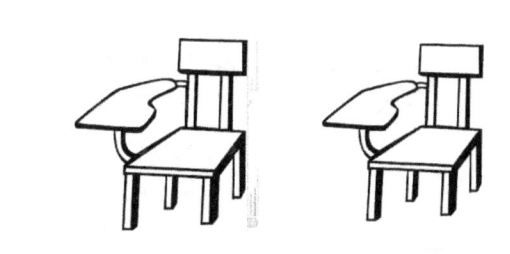
Circle the left chair

Circle the right frog

Animals Facing Left and Right Position

Which is left and which is right?

Circle all the worms facing left.

Circle all the rats facing right.

Circle all the fish facing right.

Circle all the hens facing left.

Circle all the ducks facing right.

Circle all the dogs facing left.

Circle all the flies facing left.

Measuring Up!

Capacity

We can measure capacity. When we measure the capacity of a container, we find out how much it can hold.

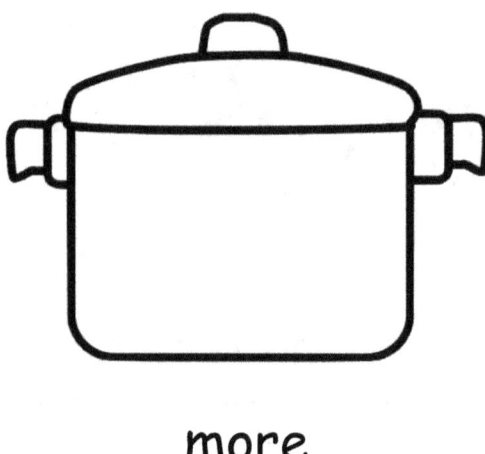

more

less

The pot can hold **more** than the glass. It has a greater capacity.

The glass holds **less** than the pot. Its capacity is less.

Weight

When we measure the weight of something, we find out how heavy it is.

The elephant is **heavier** than the frog.

The frog is **lighter** than the elephant.

lighter   heavier

Height

When we measure the height of something,
we find out how far it is
from the bottom to the top.
We find out how **tall** the object is.

The giraffe is **taller**
than the boy.

The boy is
shorter than
the giraffe.

Width

When we measure the width of something, we find out how far it is from one side to the other. We find out how **wide** it is.

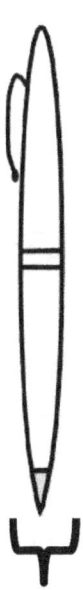

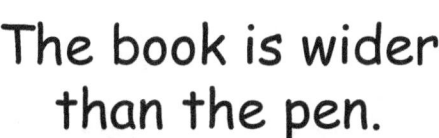

The book is wider than the pen.

The pen is narrower than the book.

Length

When we measure the length of something, we find out how far it is from one end to the other end. We find out how **long** the object is.

The school bus is **longer** than the car.

The car is **shorter** than the school bus.

The ruler is **longer** than the pencil.

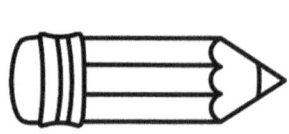 

The pencil is **shorter** than the ruler.

Color the container with the **greater** capacity.

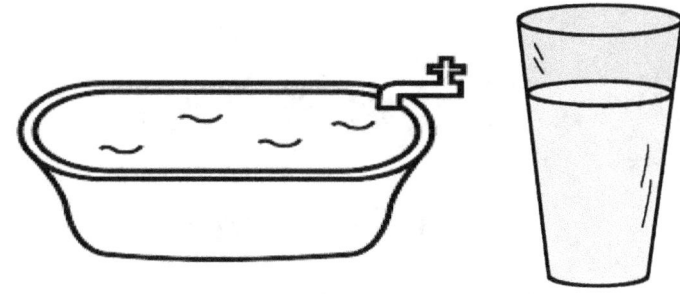

Color the object that is **wider**.

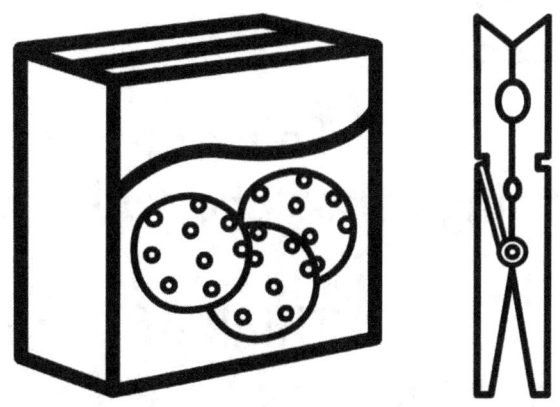

Color the object that is **longer**.

Think & Talk

How fast can you think of an answer?

Think of three
things that are **taller** than a car.

Think of three
things that are **heavier** than a crayon.

Think of three
things that are **wider** than a doorway.

Think of three
things that are **lighter** than a shoe.

Think of three
things that are **longer** than your arm.

Comparing Objects Size

Look at the objects in all four squares. Color the small object red. Color the big object brown.

Big & Small

Biggest

Color the biggest animal.

Smallest

Color the smallest animal.

Use the word list and write each word in the correct category.

How many are in each category?

Non-living

Food

Animals

cake
pea
car
hen
lotion
bag
rat
carrot

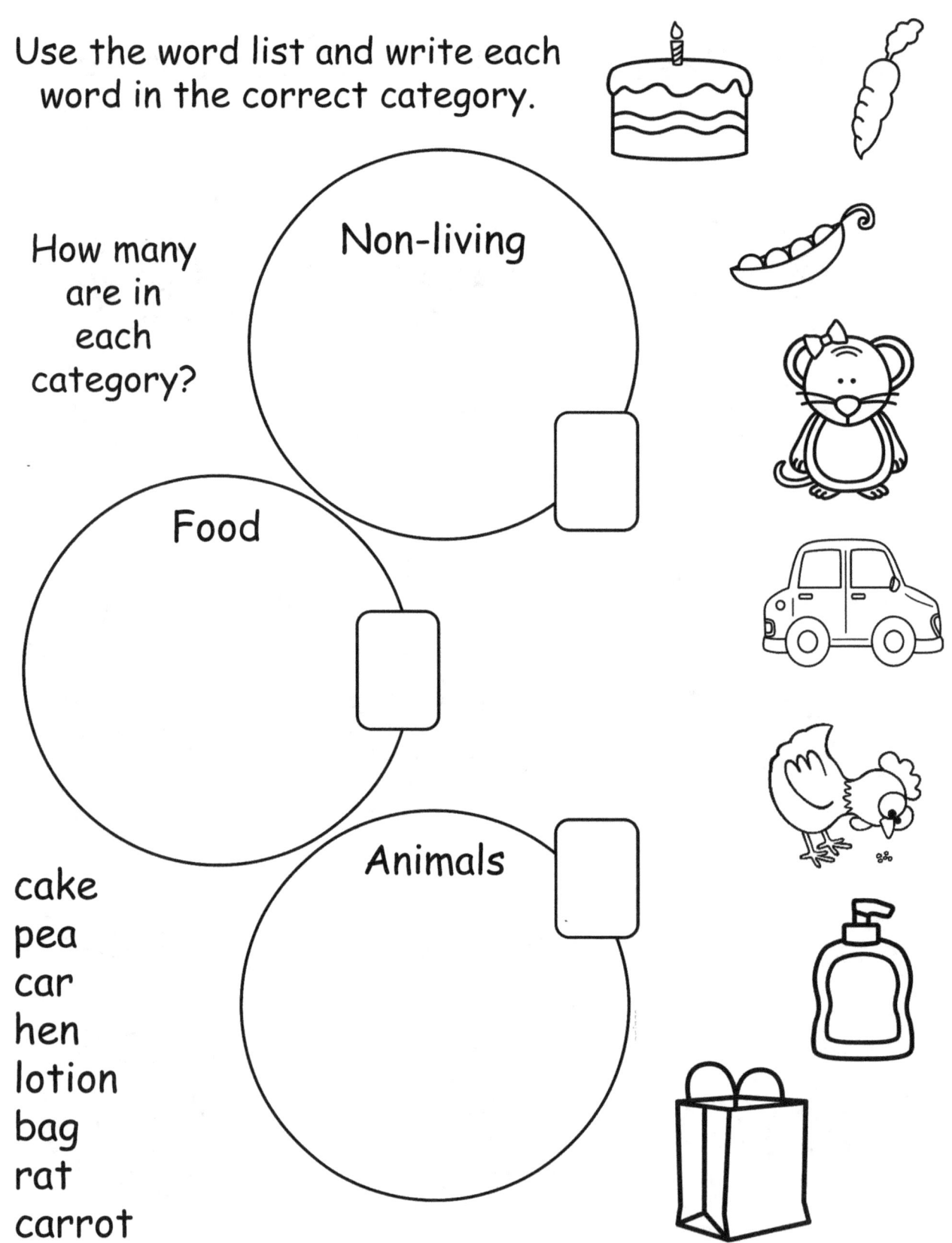

Problem Solving

Choose your answer by drawing a circle around the picture.

Tell why.

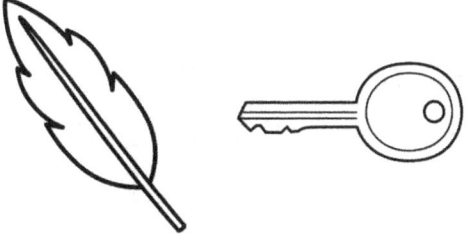

What should I tie to the end of my balloon string to keep it from floating away: a feather or a key?

If a pig and a frog were on the seesaw, whose side would touch the ground?

When packing a bag, which should you put in the bottom of the basket: eggs or pineapple?

Choose your answer by drawing a circle around the picture.

Then tell why.

Papa needs to get something from the top shelf of the closet. Which ladder should he use?

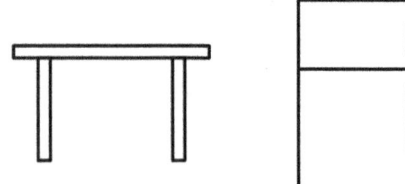

Zaq wants to keep his candy away from his little brother. Should he put it on the table or on top of the refrigerator?

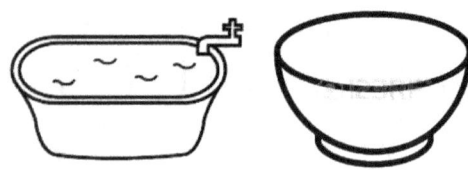

Momo wants to give his tiny turtle a bath. Should he use the pan or the bathtub?

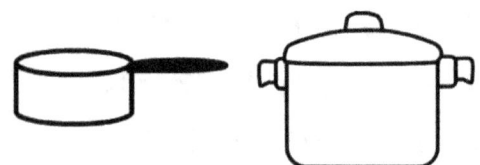

Mama is having a big party. She is going to cook jollof rice. Which pot should she use?

Musu needs to make a bridge to cross a stream. Should she use a log or a rock?

Time

60 seconds = 1 minute
60 minutes = 1 hour
24 hours = 1 day
7 days = 1 week
52 weeks = 1 year
365 days = 1 year
Decade = 10 years
Century = 100 years

All About Time

We measure **time** using a clock.

Analog Clock

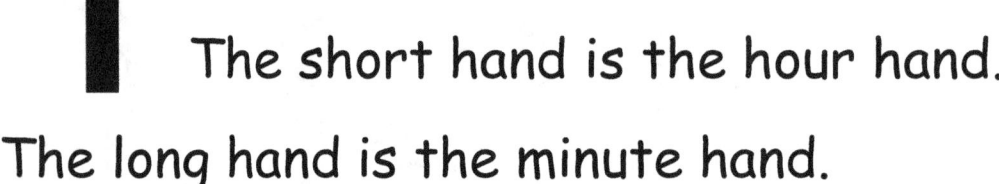

The short hand is the hour hand.
The long hand is the minute hand.

30 minutes = a half hour

The minute hand is at 6 when it is half an hour.

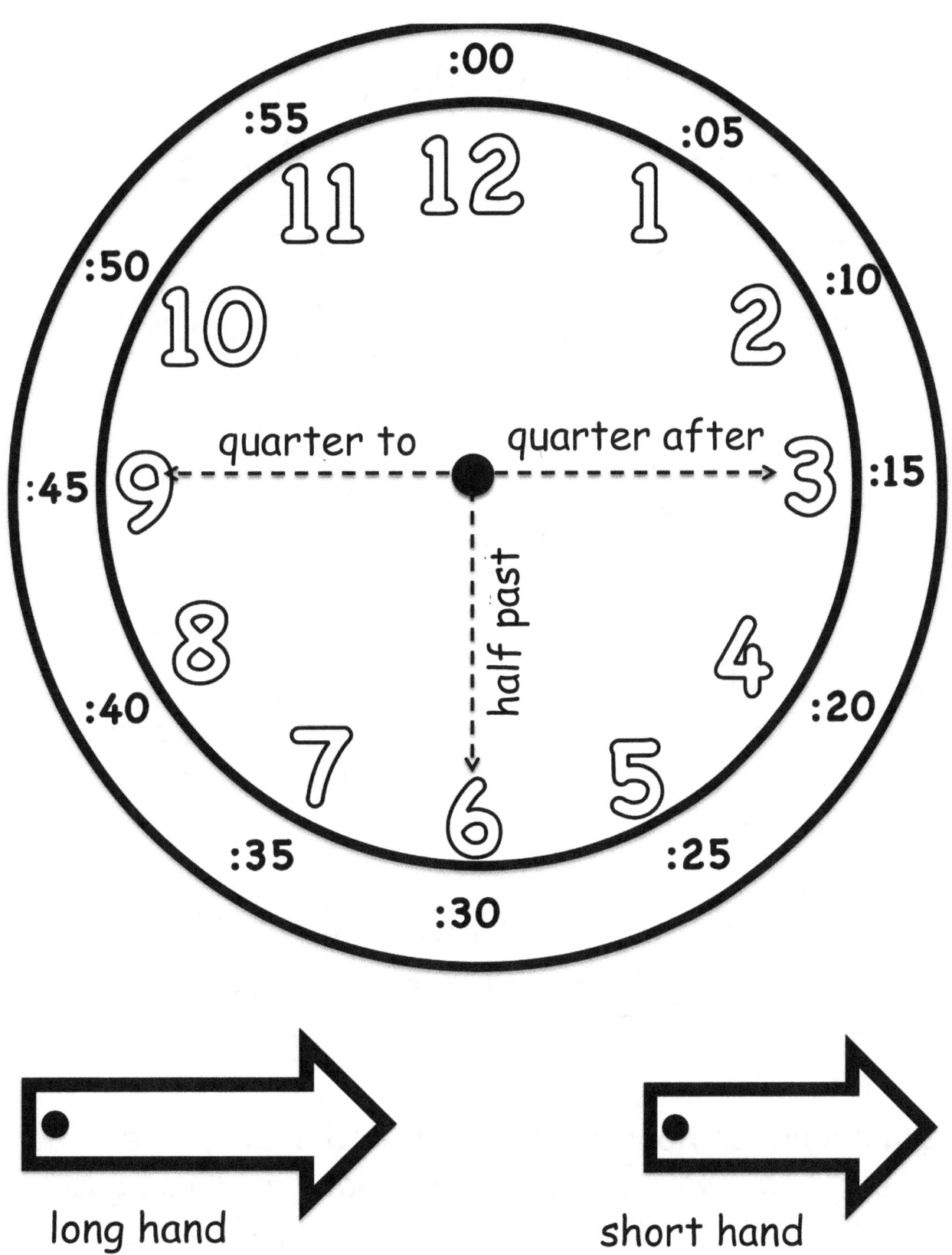

Telling Time

Step 1
Hour Hand

Look at the short hand, what it's passed and stop!

Step 2
Minute Hand

2:05

Look at the long hand, start at 12 and count by 5's.

What time is it?
It is 5 minutes passed 2.

I'm a smaller hour hand, short and stout, I tell the hour and give a shout. I'm a longer minute hand, big and tall, I tell the minute and that's all.

What Time is it?

What time is it?

Tic Toc   Draw the Clock!

Draw the hands on the clock to show the time.

3:00

11:00

6:30

9:30

2:00

8:30

Digital Clock

On a digital clock, o'clock = :00

Half past the hour is :30

What time is it?

_____   _____   _____

Word Problems

What's the problem?
For each problem,
write a number to solve it.

Addition

| Sapo read 3 books on Monday and 2 books on Tuesday. How many books did Sapo read? | |

| Korlu borrowed 1 book from the library and Musu borrowed 3 books. How many books did they borrow all together? | |

| I have 2 big books and 2 little books. How many books do I have? | |

| Zaq had 3 red crayons and 1 blue crayon. How many crayons does Zaq have? | |

| I saw 4 oranges fall, then I saw 1 more. How many oranges did I see? | |

| I saw 4 trucks drive by, then 1 more. How many trucks did I see? | |

Take Away

| I made 3 paper books. I gave 1 to my friend. How many paper books do I have now? | |

| There are 5 boys sitting at the table and then 4 stood up. How many boys are sitting? | |

| Ballah had 4 books and he gave 2 to his sister. How many books does he have now? | |

I had 5 pieces of milk candy. I ate 2. How many pieces do I have now?	
I see 4 frogs in the yard. 2 jumped away. How many frogs are left?	
I see 3 fish and all 3 swam away. How many fish do I see now?	
I had 4 dollars. I spent 2 on a toy. How many dollars do I have now?	
Mama bought 3 lollipops. She gave me 1 lollipop and gave Musu 1. How many lollipops does Mama have left?	
Momo got 5 cars for his birthday. He gave 1 car to Zaq. How many cars does Momo have now?	
Grandma gave Zaq two bananas. He gave 1 to his little sister. How many does Zaq have left?	

I Can Show My Thinking

Use tally marks to solve the equations.

| Read. | 4 + 5 = 10 |

Is the sum correct?
How do you know. Solve.

[ ]

The answer was

| Read. | 1 + 9 = 10 |

Is the sum correct?
How do you know. Solve.

[ ]

The answer was

Use tally marks to solve the equations.

| Read. | 2 + 7 = 8 |

Is the sum correct?
How do you know. Solve.

The answer was

| Read. | 4 + 2 = 9 |

Is the sum correct?
How do you know. Solve.

The answer was

Use tally marks to solve the equations.

| Read. | $5 + 5 = 10$ |

Is the sum correct?
How do you know. Solve.

The answer was

| Read. | $3 + 6 = 8$ |

Is the sum correct?
How do you know. Solve.

The answer was

Use tally marks to solve the equations.

| Read. | 1 + 7 = 9 |

Is the sum correct?
How do you know. Solve.

The answer was

| Read. | 10 + 0 = 10 |

Is the sum correct?
How do you know. Solve.

The answer was

Use tally marks to solve the equations.

Read. 2 - 1 = 1

Is the difference correct?
How do you know. Solve.

The answer was

Read. 9 - 3 = 6

Is the difference correct?
How do you know. Solve.

The answer was

Use tally marks to solve the equations.

| Read. | 10 - 1 = 9 |

Is the difference correct?
How do you know. Solve.

[ ]

The answer was

| Read. | 10 - 5 = 4 |

Is the difference correct?
How do you know. Solve.

The answer was

Use tally marks to solve the equations.

Read. $3 - 3 = 0$

Is the difference correct?
How do you know. Solve.

The answer was

Read. $4 - 1 = 3$

Is the difference correct?
How do you know. Solve.

The answer was

Use tally marks to solve the equations.

Read.   6 - 3 = 5

Is the difference correct?
How do you know. Solve.

The answer was

Read.   5 - 2 = 4

Is the difference correct?
How do you know. Solve.

The answer was

Color and Count

How many?

Comparing Amounts

Count the eggs. Write the number. Circle the number that is greater.

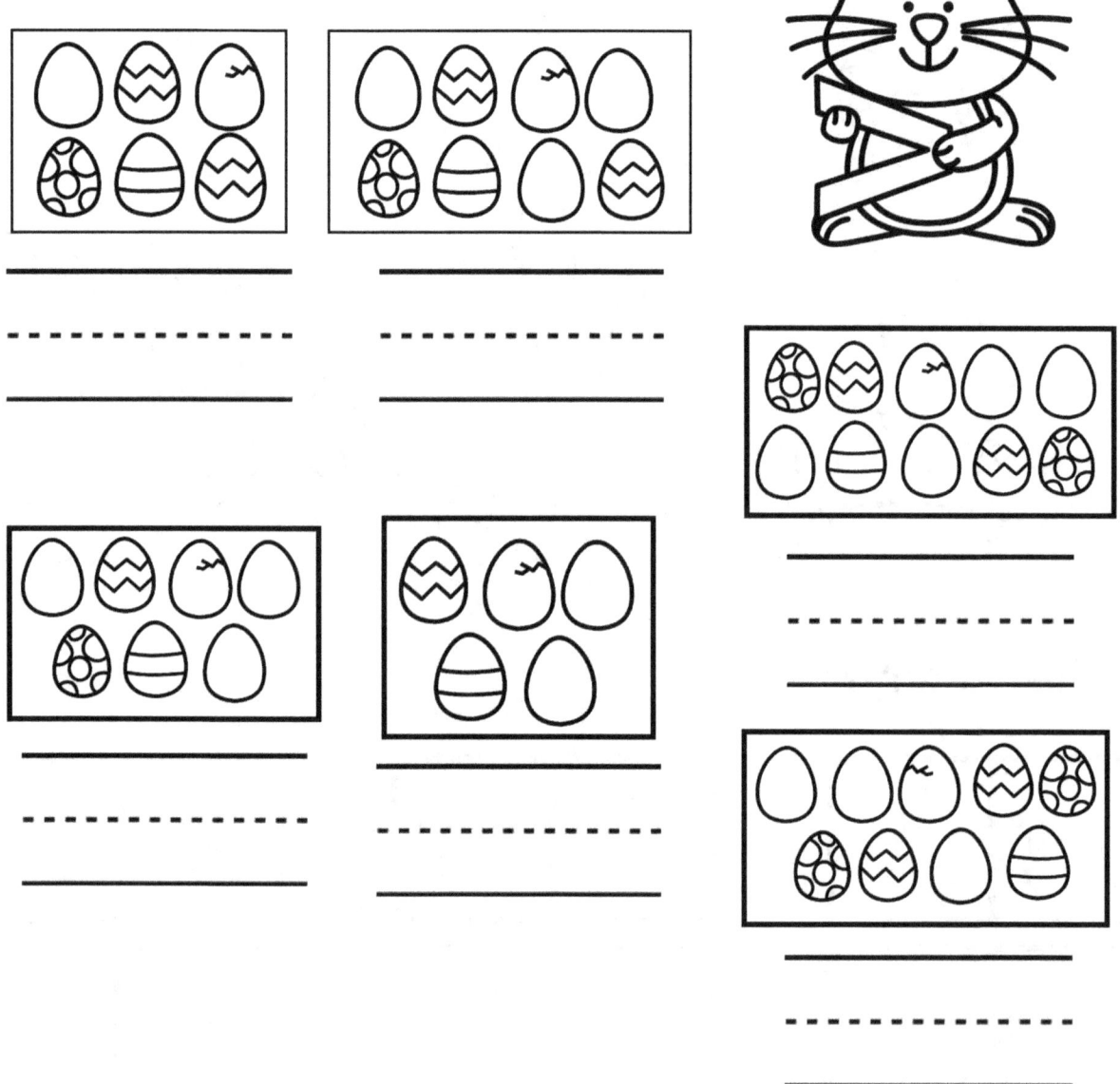

Color and Count

How many?

Before and After Numbers 10-30

Write the numbers that come **before** and **after**.

14 15 16

___ 17 ___   ___ 22 ___

___ 11 ___   ___ 13 ___

___ 25 ___   ___ 28 ___

___ 19 ___   ___ 21 ___

More tomatoes to add.

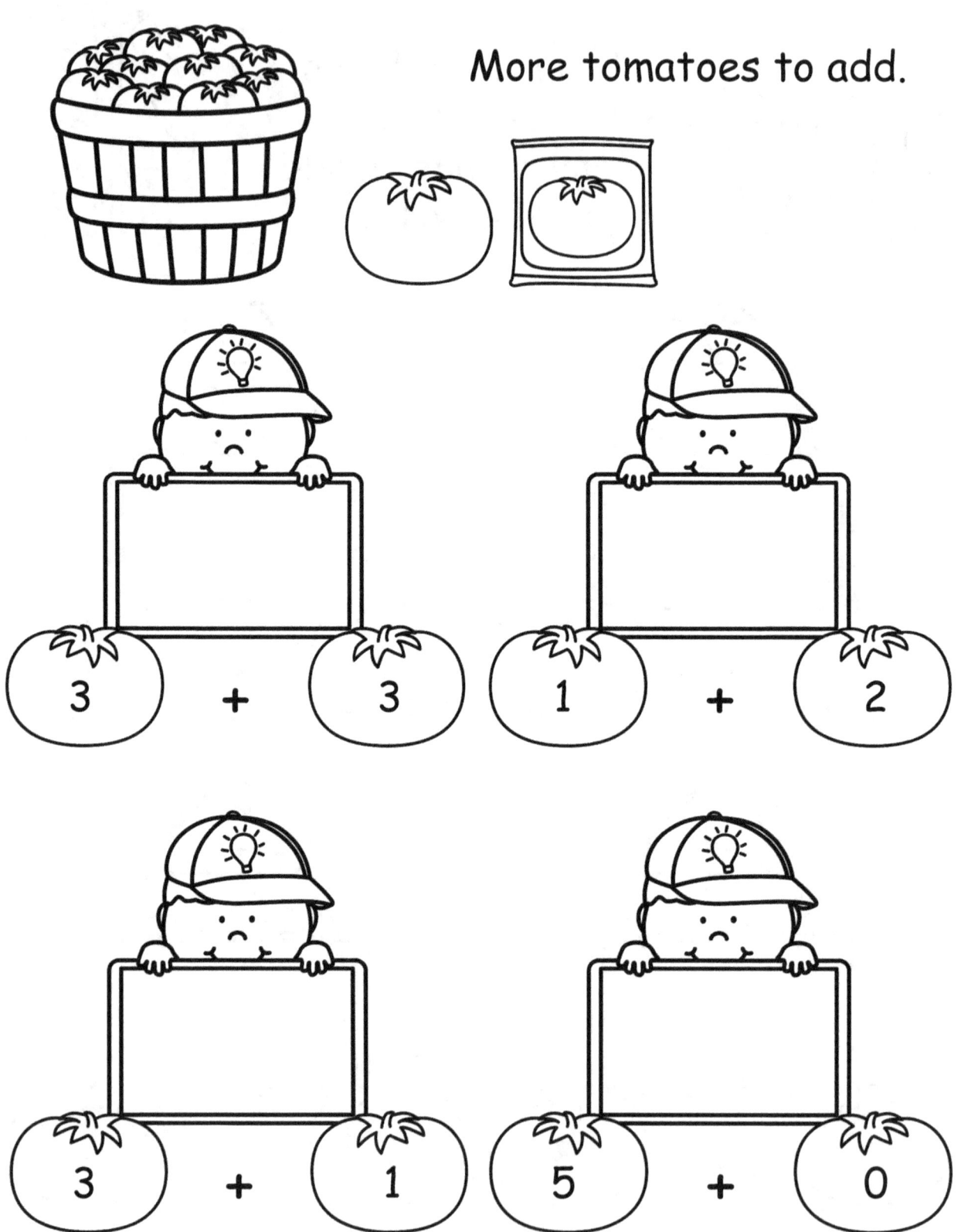

Draw a line to connect the numbers to the correct boxes.

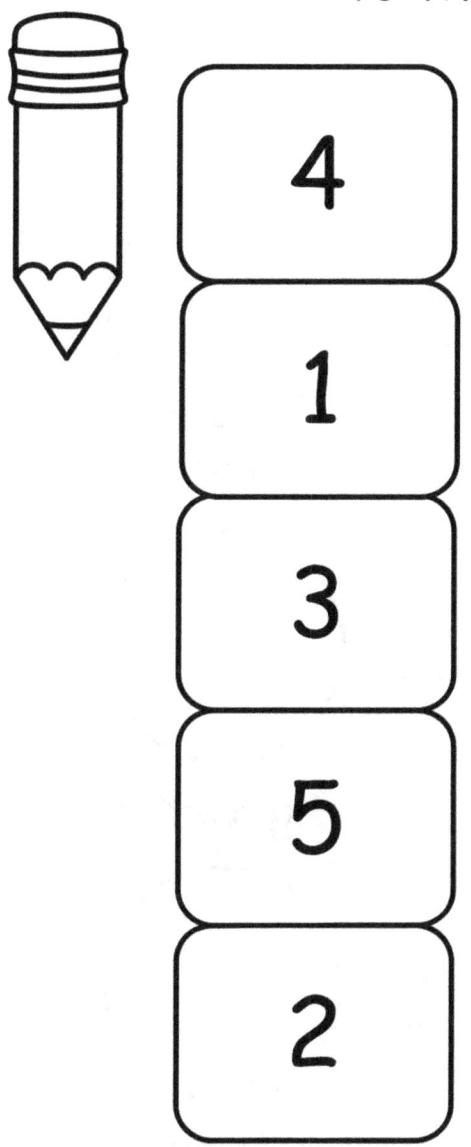
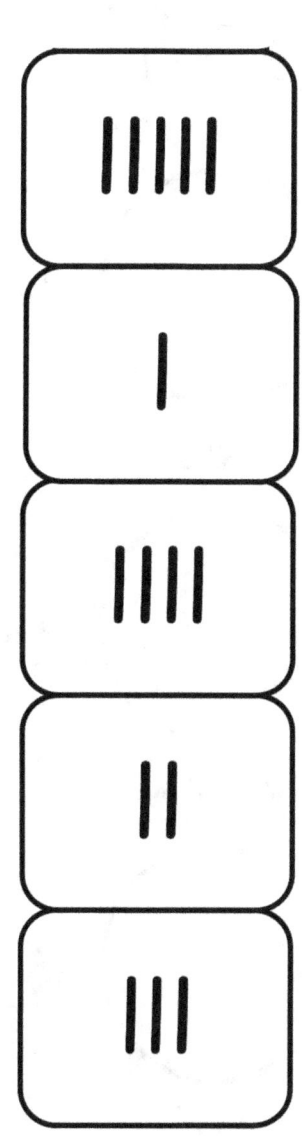

Primary Color Mixing

Color the circles.

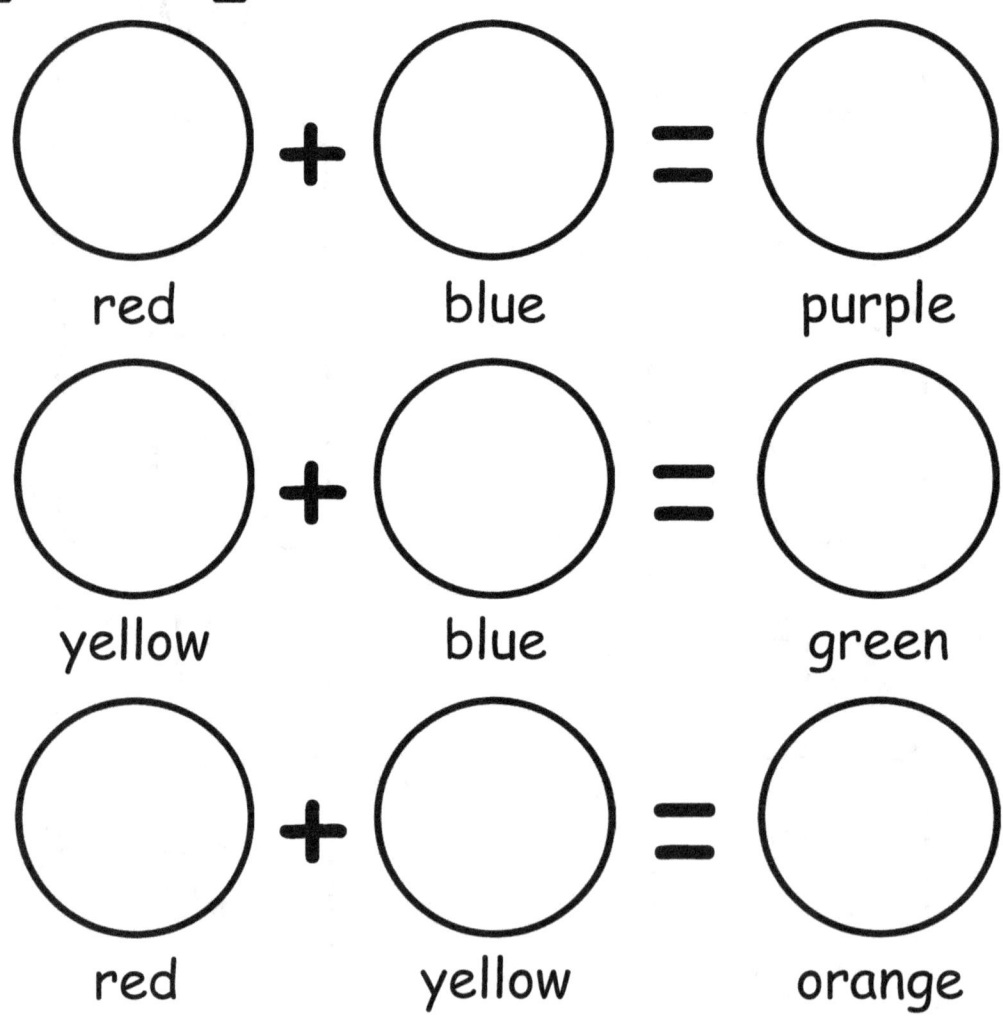

154

Money

We save our money at the bank.

Ellen Johnson-Sirleaf is Liberia's first elected female president. She worked at the World Bank before she became president.

Currency & Money

| LRD (L$) & USD ($) |

Currency includes coins and paper bills

Liberian Dollar by name and value

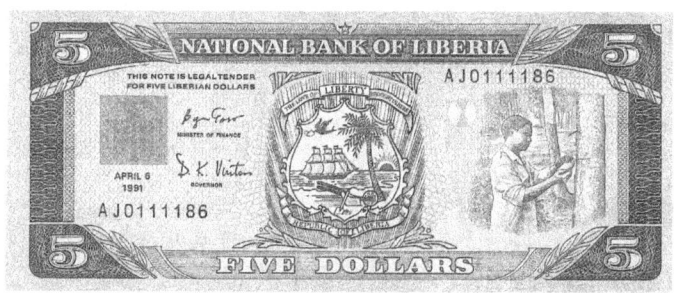 L$5

 L$10

 L$20

 L$50

Word Problems With LRDs (L$)

Momo has a $5 bill and a $10 bill. How much money does he have?

Papa gave Hawa a $5 bill, a $10 bill, and a $20 bill. How much money does Hawa have?

Fatu has $20. She buys a candy bar for $5. How much money does she have left?

Korlu bought a keychain for $10 and a book for $20. How much money did she spend?

Momo has a $10 bill and a $20 bill. How much money does he have?

Mama gave Hawa 2 $5 bills, a $10 bill, and a $20 bill. How much money does Hawa have?

Fatu has $50. She buys a dress for $20. How much money does she have left?

Zaq took $50 to the store with him. He spent $10 on a pack of gum. How much money does Zaq have now?

Mama took $50 to the market with her. She spent $10 on a bottle of palm oil and $20 on a cup of rice. How much money does Mama have now?

Marie went to the bookstore. She purchased an eraser for $5 and a pencil for $10. How much money should she give the cashier?

Papa took $40 to the store with him. He spent $10 on a pack of nails. How much money does Papa have now?

Momo gave Hawa $5. Fatu give Hawa $10. Korlu gave Hawa $20. Mama gave Hawa $5. How much money does Hawa have?

Coins and Bills

Penny, penny, penny, easily spent.
Copper brown and worth one cent.

Nickel, nickel, thick and fat.
You're worth five cent, I know that.

Dime, dime, little and thin,
I remember you're worth ten.

Quarter, quarter, big and bold,
You're worth twenty-five I'm told.

Dollar, dollar, green and long,
With 100 cents you can't go wrong.

What We Do With Our Money

Save   Spend   Share

1¢ = 1   5¢ = 5

10¢ = 10   25¢ = 25

Save.
Save.
Save.

Write how many cents (¢) each coin is worth.

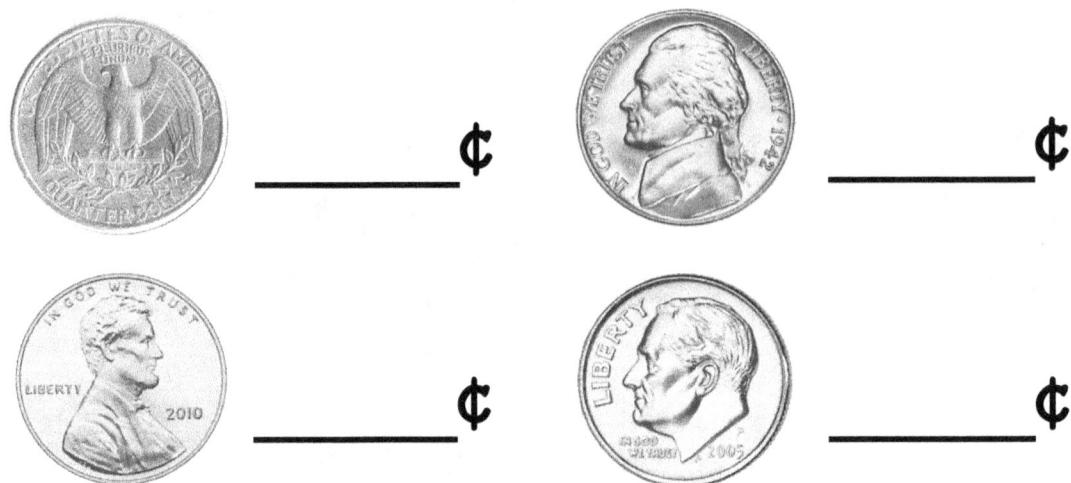

Draw a line from each coin to its name.

Penny

Dime

Nickel

Quarter

Math Crossword Puzzles

Spell the correct answer; uncover the secret word.

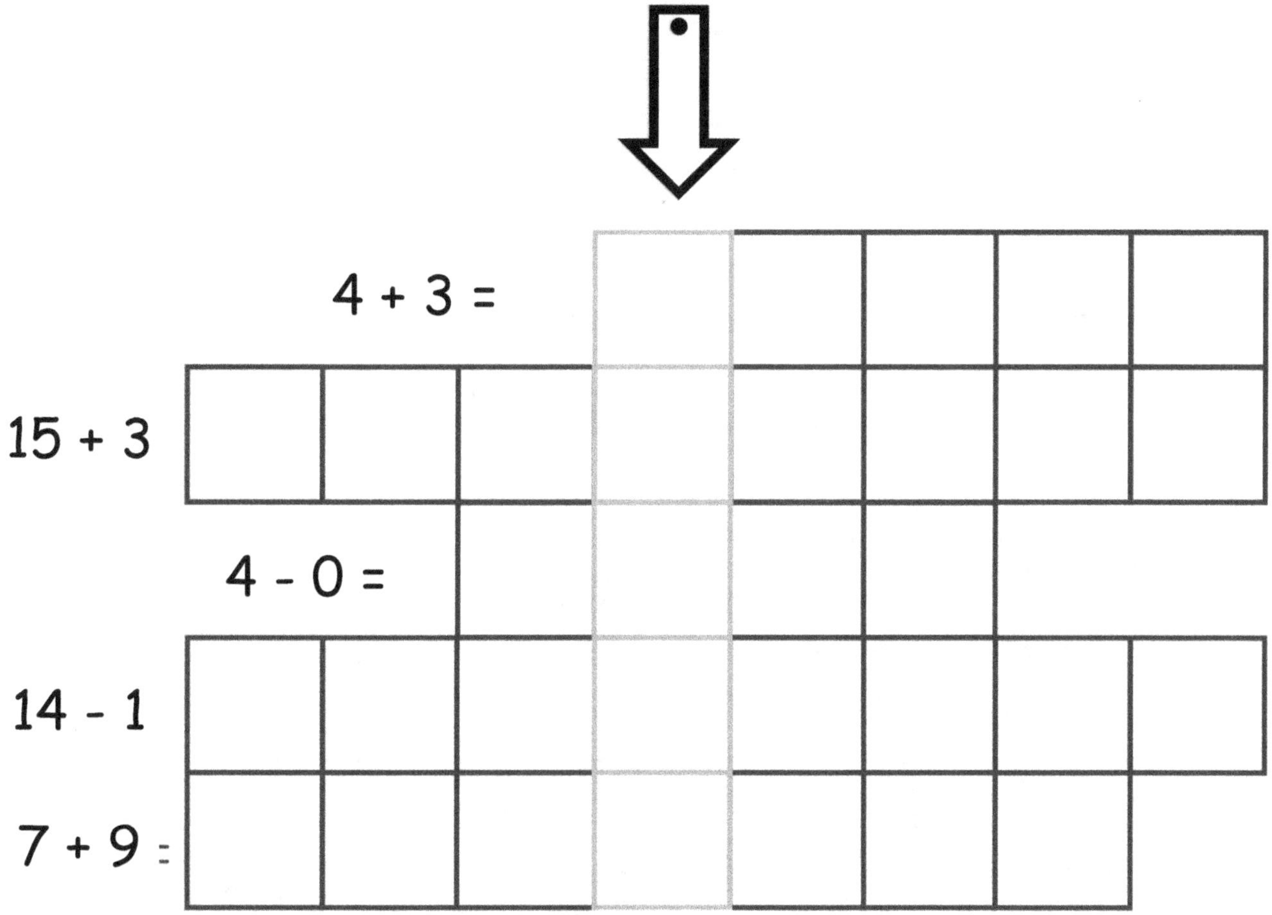

4 + 3 =

15 + 3

4 - 0 =

14 - 1

7 + 9 =

Secret Word

Spell the correct answer;
uncover the secret word.

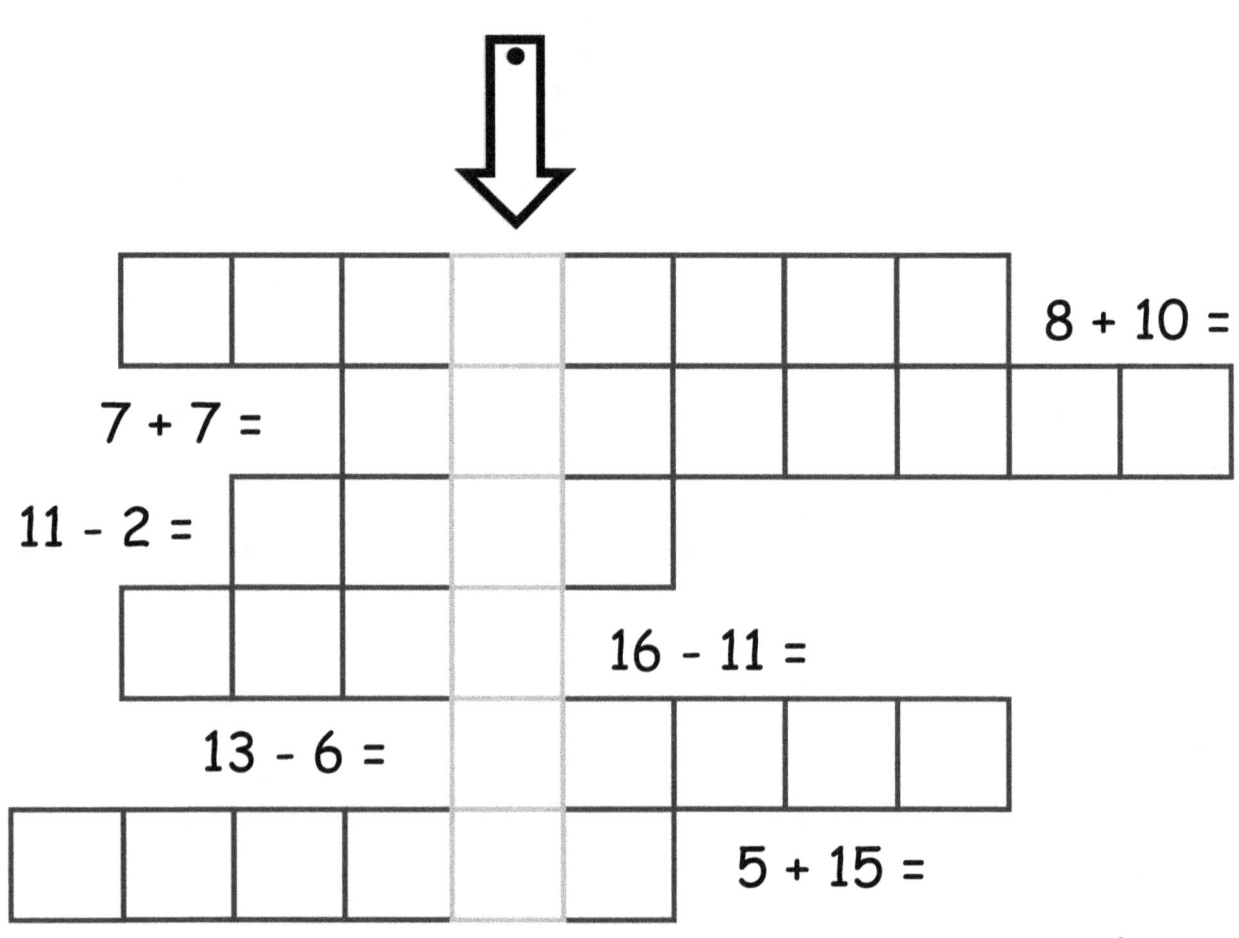

7 + 7 =
11 - 2 =
13 - 6 =
8 + 10 =
16 - 11 =
5 + 15 =

Secret Word

Spell the correct answer; uncover the secret word.

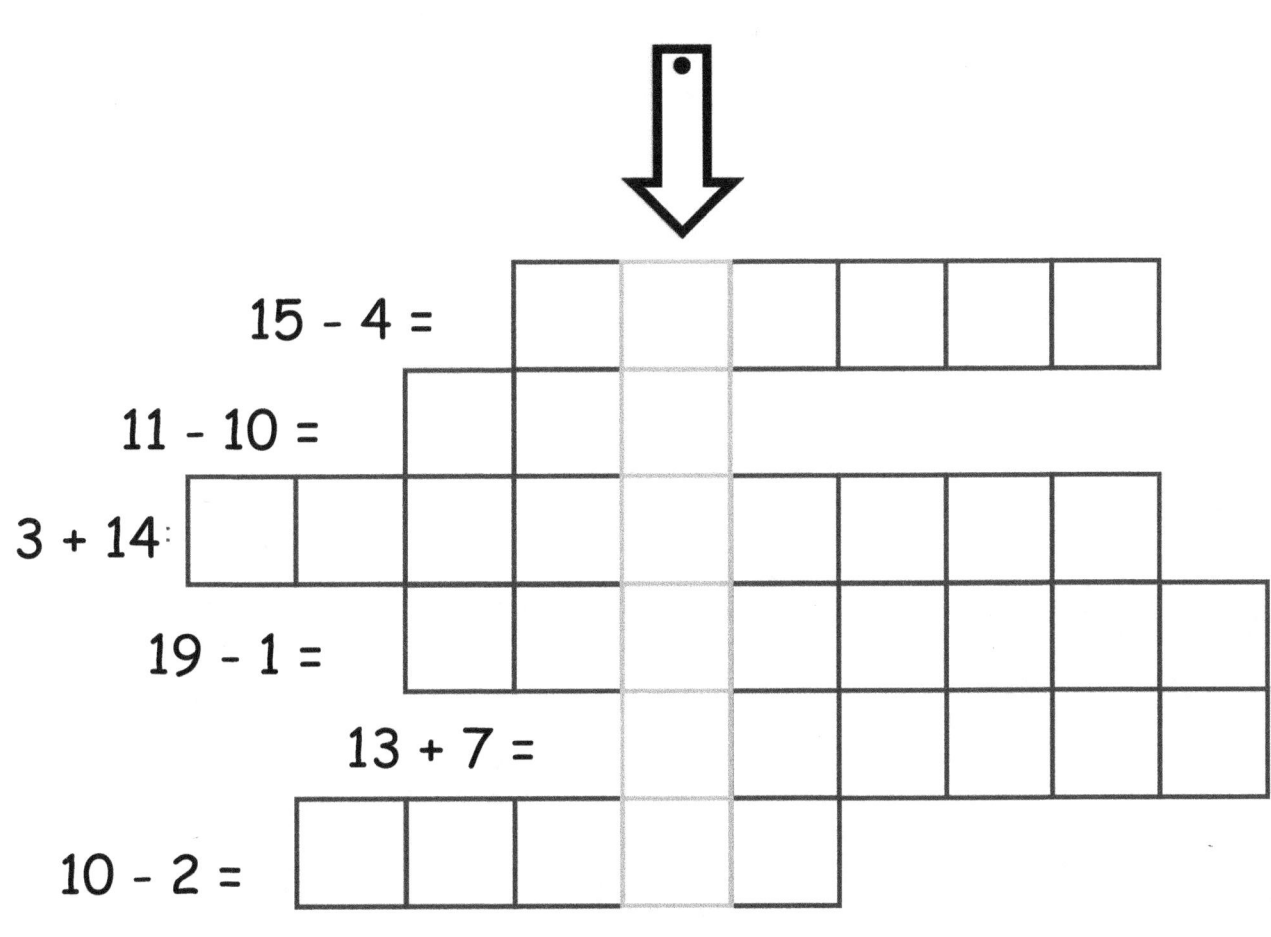

15 - 4 =
11 - 10 =
3 + 14 =
19 - 1 =
13 + 7 =
10 - 2 =

Secret Word